D0523156

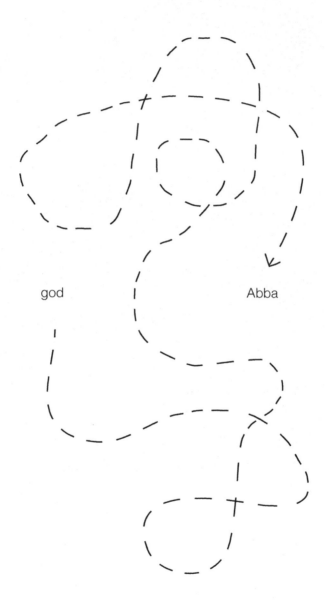

god   Abba

Moving From god to Abba

God. Us. And how we think about both.

Nate Kupish

Copyright © 2016 by Nathaniel Kupish

All rights reserved. If you would like to use material from the book, prior written permission must be obtained by contacting the author at natekupish.com. Thank you for your support of the author's rights.

Unless otherwise noted, all Scripture quotations are taken from the New International Version of the Bible. THE HOLY BIBLE, NEW INTERNATIONAL VERSION®, NIV® Copyright © 1973, 1978, 1984, 2011 by Biblica, Inc.® Used by permission. All rights reserved worldwide.

Scripture quotations also taken from The Message. Copyright © 1993, 1994, 1995, 1996, 2000, 2001, 2002. Used by permission of NavPress Publishing Group. Scripture quotations also taken from the NEW AMERICAN STANDARD BIBLE®, Copyright © 1960,1962,1963,1968,1971,1972,1973, 1975,1977,1995 by The Lockman Foundation. Used by permission.

For information about special discounts available for bulk purchases, please, contact us through natekupish.com.

Cover design and illustration by Ryan Peterson.

First Edition: April 2016

ISBN-13: 978-1530331673

ISBN-10: 1530331676

Contents

**For in Him
we *live*
and *move*
and have our being.**

Acts 17v28a

Thank You

Thank you *Brandon* and *Karlee* for editing the piles of words this was and helping shape them into what is now, *Moving From god to Abba. You help me see God through your attention to detail and desire for clarity.*

Thank you *Ryan* for the cover art and for taking me to see Mute Math the other day. You take concepts and make them visual in a way that leaves me in wonder. *You help me see God through your art and design.*

Thank you *Hillary* for being my patient partner and closest friend. For helping me think outside of good intentioned, but limiting thoughts about life with God. For taking care of me, for teaching me how to eat well, and for showing me the value in work and exercise. *You help me see God through the way you value each moment as His gift to us.*

Thank you *Brandon* for being like a brother to me. For teaching me how to listen, how to let God love me, and how to care more about people encountering God than getting them to agree with me. *You help me see God through the beauty of letting God be God.*

Thank you *Mom* for always being there. For teaching our family how to love God with our whole lives. Thank you for your constant support, availability, and patience as we worked through life stuff. *You help me see God through the way you care for me and so many others.*

Thank you *Mike and Melissa* for being our core community the past few years. *Mike,* thanks for being the most down to earth, value instilling person I know, and for setting a passcode on my phone to lock out the News app so that I wouldn't get distracted. *You help me see God through the way you love people. Melissa,* thanks for helping me be a better thinker. You ask the right questions, going deeper than the typical everyday conversation. *You help me see God through the intricacy of life and thought.*

Thank you *Evan* for championing honesty, value, and honor in me (and everyone around you). For constant encouragement in this project, and for being my friend... endlessly pastoring me towards Jesus. *You help me see God through your honest thought and liturgy.*

Thank you *Daniel* for helping me see the word "that" is a filler word and for being a very good friend in the midst of all sorts of life situations. *You help me see God through your patience and clarity.*

Thank you *Gerry* for the book suggestions about the canonicity of the Scriptures. *You help me see God through your devotion to make the Scriptures understandable to anyone who will listen.*

Thank you *Royal* (our dog) for all the morning cuddles. *You help me see God through your constant affection and love.*

And thank you *Upper Left, Barista, Good Coffee*, and *Coava* for letting me spend my Friday's in your incredible shops enjoying delicious coffee while writing. *You help me see God by making really good stuff.*

Note From the Author...
this will help as you read

Moving From god to Abba is a collection of directional thoughts aimed towards us growing in intimacy with the Father, Son, and Holy Spirit.

It's written with hopes that something in it may be of help as you're honest about figuring out life with God and people.

The word "god," used in the title of this book, is intentionally not capitalized. It notes the idea of an unknown, or unknowable *god*. Thus, we'll be exploring a possible relational shift in the way we think about God and ourselves.

Some of the ideas in this book may evolve and change over time.

They have for me.

So wrestle with them before soaking them in. I hope the way they're approached is correct and helpful for you, but I'm guessing some of it may be off. I'll never forget when years ago, my friend John Mark said something along the lines of, "At best, I'm 80% right. The problem is, I don't know what 20% I'm wrong about." But I wonder if that's part of the process... to be wrong sometimes, yet to be humble about admitting it?

Please know my tone in writing is far from *this is how it is,* and much more as if we're sitting across from each other sharing a coffee exchanging real questions and dialog about God, us, and how we think about both.

As you read, if you're inspired to create… whether that's through writing, painting, drawing, film, music, or whatever medium you most enjoy, do it! Just as four people standing around the same object would explain what they see in different ways… my perspective, experiences, and interpretations of God, the Scriptures, and the world around us are far from the full picture. We need each other and Holy Spirit to move us into deeper understandings of what He's like.

You may notice I leave out "the" when referring to *Holy Spirit.* While most modern English translations of the Bible include it, our interpretation of what "the" means can have a negative affect on the way we think about God. The hope for leaving it out is to remember He's relational, not a force.

He loves you *so* much.

May you continue to know His delight *for you* as you read.

Nate

Preface

What if life with God is more like a walk than a test? And what if it's less about *answers* and more about *enjoying*?

—

2,650 miles.

That's the distance of the Pacific Crest Trail which stretches from Mexico, up through California, Oregon, Washington, and ends in Canada.

Many have done parts, but only a small handful have hiked the entire trail in one go.

And like those people trying to explain to the rest of us what it was like to live in the forest for six months, hiking countless hours a day in the silence and beauty of creation... I'd suggest there are few ways to make brief summaries of the big questions we work through in life. Often, stories and illustrations do a better job.

So for the sake of thinking about it in fresh ways, let's say *life with God* resembles a long hike. And along the way, a few major questions are sure to arise between you and Him and the people you're with. You may ask how to do it well. How to make it count. Possibly even wondering at times why you chose to set out in the first place.

We'll come to places where our fears have to be dealt with. Moments that will force us to choose whether to press on or to turn back.

Some will call it quits for a time… missing out on the sights, sounds, and feelings just ahead. For them, another part of the trail is their next step, maybe returning to what's comfortable and seemingly safe. But others will pause as the breeze blows past their face and in a moment of deep connection to something more than themselves, will experience a moment that cannot be adequately captured by words.

This book is intended to be like meeting a stranger along that trail (regardless of which direction you're walking) who offers you a spot next to the fire, a warm meal, and a place to rest before moving on. One friendly face to talk with among the many you'll encounter along the way. I have no hidden agenda or propaganda. I simply want to encourage you on your journey of life with God and share what I've seen and learned in hopes to propel you further, feeling more honest and healthy as you continue on.

The chapters aren't perfect, and funny enough this became intentional. There may be loose ends and plenty of questions left open for you to work through with others… but I think that's a healthy way to approach this kind of subject. In humility, we come to God and each other open to the fact we don't have it all together. I have my own stuff. Call them trials, struggles, temptations, or the demonic… the fact is, it all points to stuff only God can heal.

The Father, Jesus, and Holy Spirit are the point of this book.

So if you long to experience God in an organic, natural, and deep way, then this is for you. Or if you desperately want to believe there is a God. Or if you grew up in a church community and left. Or if deep down, you want freedom from the cycles you've started hating yourself for… this is for you.

Enjoy the time you get to spend in these pages, but balance it with being in the Scriptures. Hopefully everything written here is simply a digestion and regurgitation, by experience, of the very things in the Bible. No new thoughts, just fresh ways of communicating it. All the ideas and thoughts you'll read here are simply out-workings of experiencing the world God illuminates in His story.

His Kingdom is *here,* scattered among us like color spilling through a prism. That was a major part of the good news Jesus came to show and tell us about. Every healing, whether inner or outer, is heaven invading earth and we get to live in the place of connection with God as we welcome His healing back into our spheres of life.

I want to do what Jesus did and actually take what He said as the truth, not be in some Jesus club where I know the inside scoop. I actually want to experience Him, and because of that, I'm willing to peel back all the well-intentioned layers in order to start over with God, us, and how we think about both.

You get to set the pace at which you'll read through this, but as an encouragement, don't get fixated on the map… make the journey.

Read… yes, but then do.

Read… yes, but then pray. At the core, regardless of method or style, prayer is *both* talking and listening to God. Flowing from presence awareness (choosing to be alive to His nearness), words then follow.

The words in this book aren't written for knowledge sake. They're not here to make you smarter, "more holy," or into a "better person." They're expressions of certain core elements of life with God… or better put, just *life*.

You'll come across things to wrestle with, other things to receive, and still others that we'll call *Rhythms of Practicing Peace*. More on that in a few pages.

But above all, I really do hope you take time to slow down and listen to His voice as you lean into what He's saying to you. His love for you is unending and available for you to experience right now. Don't let your past define your future. When we say *yes* to Jesus, our past is no longer an issue for God, so it shouldn't be an issue for us either. He's the God of new things, the best things. The bread on His table is always fresh, always available to us as we come like children to simply delight in Him. He's excited about showing you more of what He's like so that you can live a more stable, more content, and more restful life.[1]

You can ask Him to become more real to you.

Then wait...

Be still...

Just breathe, choosing to be okay with whatever comes next.

So often we assume we know how He should respond. But He knows what we've said and is keenly aware of our situation.

There's nothing you've done, or could do, that can make Him stop loving you: "For I am convinced that neither death nor life, neither angels nor demons, neither the present nor the future, nor any powers, neither height nor depth, nor anything else in all creation, will be able to separate us from the love of God that is in Christ Jesus our Lord." Romans 8v38-39

He cannot love you any more... it's 100% all the time. You may be a middle schooler, college student, business person, stay at home parent, or find yourself in prison... and even still, it makes no difference. You are loved. Since your first breath, He's been whispering a lullaby of victory over your life just waiting for you to receive it. You're invited into His family and the ultimate gift of Him with you, Holy Spirit, is always available.

"But when the set time had fully come, God sent his Son, born of a woman, born under the law, to redeem those under the law, that we might receive adoption to sonship. Because you are his sons, God sent the Spirit of his Son into our hearts, the Spirit who calls out, "Abba, Father." So you are no longer a slave, but God's child; and since you are his child, God has made you also an heir." Galatians 4v4-7

So that's what we're after. A receiving and greater awareness of His presence, love, and freedom.

All of life begins with this simple, yet profound reality. An every minute, honest, and deeply secure relationship with our Father, His Son, and Holy Spirit. A 24/7 give and take, back and forth, conversational kind of relationship.

He longs for you to make Him your safe place. The place you live from. Your energy source. The standard by which you run every thought and movement through. His name is Holy Spirit, and in Him you'll find true fulfillment for your everyday moments. He offers fullness that has the ability to heal all situations across all cultures and contexts. A confidence that pushes back the discouragement. A peace that's far beyond trite statements of self-reflection or calmness. Deeper than words can express.

In his book *The Pastor*, Eugene Peterson says, "The artist has eyes to connect the visible and the invisible and the skill to show complete what we in our inattentive distractions see only in bits and pieces."[2]

Just like that, David who himself was an artist, used words as paint to create masterpieces on the canvas of his own soul. He constantly reminded himself of who God was for him. Psalm 31 is one of my favorite expressions of our unseen surroundings David gives us. It beautifully expresses the concept of God as our refuge, our hiding place, and our safe place.

Psalm 31:

"In you, Lord, I have taken refuge;
let me never be put to shame;
deliver me in your righteousness.

Turn your ear to me,
come quickly to my rescue;
be my rock of refuge,
a strong fortress to save me.
Since you are my rock and my fortress,
for the sake of your name lead and guide me.
Keep me free from the trap that is set for me,
for you are my refuge.
Into your hands I commit my spirit;
deliver me, Lord, my faithful God.

I hate those who cling to worthless idols;
as for me, I trust in the Lord.
I will be glad and rejoice in your love,
for you saw my affliction
and knew the anguish of my soul.
You have not given me into the hands of the enemy
but have set my feet in a spacious place.

Be merciful to me, Lord, for I am in distress;
my eyes grow weak with sorrow,
my soul and body with grief.
My life is consumed by anguish
and my years by groaning;
my strength fails because of my affliction,
and my bones grow weak.
Because of all my enemies,
I am the utter contempt of my neighbors
and an object of dread to my closest friends–
those who see me on the street flee from me.
I am forgotten as though I were dead;
I have become like broken pottery.
For I hear many whispering,
"Terror on every side!"
They conspire against me
and plot to take my life.

But I trust in you, Lord;

I say, "You are my God."
My times are in your hands;
deliver me from the hands of my enemies,
from those who pursue me.
Let your face shine on your servant;
save me in your unfailing love.
Let me not be put to shame, Lord,
for I have cried out to you;
but let the wicked be put to shame
and be silent in the realm of the dead.
Let their lying lips be silenced,
for with pride and contempt
they speak arrogantly against the righteous.

How abundant are the good things
that you have stored up for those who fear you,
that you bestow in the sight of all,
on those who take refuge in you.
In the shelter of your presence you hide them
from all human intrigues;
you keep them safe in your dwelling
from accusing tongues.

Praise be to the Lord,
for he showed me the wonders of his love
when I was in a city under siege.
In my alarm I said,
"I am cut off from your sight!"
Yet you heard my cry for mercy
when I called to you for help.

Love the Lord, all his faithful people!
The Lord preserves those who are true to him,
but the proud he pays back in full.
Be strong and take heart,
all you who hope in the Lord."

He is *for you.*

This book is intended to be a kind of invitation or request... like being asked on a second date, then a third, with the increasing feeling that something amazing is unfolding between you and Him. It's the setting of a space for you to see Him from different angles. Everything beautiful you've experienced in life is like a drop in the ocean of who He is and He's giddy to show you more. The God who knows your name has been singing songs of victory, rest, and love over you ever since you were young.

He says, "Come to me and I'll give you a resting place." Matthew 11v28

So this is the place we'll start from. The foundation and the fuel for everything we'll talk about. Relationship with Him. As in really knowing Him, to the degree of inexpressible interaction. This is the life He welcomes us into, Himself.

This isn't a rigid theology book only some can understand, it's a simple heart book open to everyone regardless of where you're at along the journey. It's about growing in the ability to hear His tone of joy over you. It's about learning to see His smile when He thinks about you. It's about breaking the lies of who you think He is and replacing them with the truth, picking up your rightful identity based on His thoughts about you.[3] It's about learning to sink deeply into unending living conversation and bliss with the person of Jesus. The God man. The One who redeemed, and is redeeming, every one of your broken situations, relationships, ways of thinking that don't work, physical pains, emotional hurts, and desires that have left you needing more.

That's why He's the fulfillment you're longing for... because somewhere in all of us, we know things aren't right. We know something's off. We all see it, but it can take a moment of tenderness to admit it. This is why Jesus is so moving to me. He's everything we wish could be true.

Throughout these pages there will be a handful of what I call *Rhythms of Practicing Peace*. Here's a quick introduction to *what* they are, *how* they work, and *why* they're really helpful in our life with God.

Let's start with *why*.

If you and I are anything alike, forgetfulness happens.

I often forget my keys are in the ignition of my car as I grab my bag, lock the doors, and head inside. It's not until the next morning while I'm looking for them that I realize where I'd left them. Hillary gives me a cute little grin on those mornings that says, "Babe, did you check the ignition?" She knows me well. I've learned I need a reminder to take my keys with me when I get out of the car which is why there's a sticky note on the inside of my car window.

There's a ton of similarity between that situation and life with God. We read a line like in Romans 8 about how nothing can separate us from God's love, but then we feel distant at times. Why is that? My guess isn't demons. Rather, it's simply because we forget what's true. We all need reminders, just like the sticky note in my car that reminds me to take my keys with me. Reminders of what God says about us can be extremely helpful and even change the way we think and act.

So that's the *why…* because we need reminders.

Now the *what.*

Rhythms like these are a regular part of my life. Some daily, others once a week or month, and still others are for special geographic places. Places of rest and retreat, of shalom.

Please know there's no schedule or calendar to follow. They're relational, not task oriented. The rhythms you'll read in these pages are simply a few of my own, but as you learn the framework, I'd encourage you to create ones that make sense to you… and be sure to share them with people.

They're practical, active, and simple ways to slow down and recenter our minds, perspectives, wills, and emotions onto the One who is ahead and behind us.[4]

I'd encourage you to live in the freedom of finding what works best *for you* as you grow in patterns of enjoying life with God.

Here's *how* they work.

Let's try one.

—

Rhythm of Practicing Peace

You may want to read through this once, then set it aside, clear your lap and hands, close your eyes (for distraction sake), and walk through it again.

Take a minute to slow down.

Breathe in...

Then out.

When you're ready, keep reading.

Picture yourself in a moment when you realize you just messed up, you did something you knew wasn't God's best. Your face is looking down at your feet and your shoulders are heavy. You're so overwhelmed by guilt that your knees feel weak, your stomach upset, and you just wish you could disappear. So aware of your failure that it feels as tangible as the clothes on your back. You hear a voice telling you to give up, that you're a screw up and never going to be a person of soundness or clarity. That you're dirty and God wants nothing to do with you.

Now look up... Jesus is standing closer than you realized. His eyes of fire[5] see through your emotions of shame and guilt because in His mind, they've already been dealt with. His eyes track with yours as a smile breaks across His face. He begins to sing over you, a song of healing and restoring for all that's been lost. You realize the condemning voice you'd heard moments earlier wasn't His, it was another voice. His is not timid or sly, but gentle and full of authority and honor.

As you look at His hands you notice He's holding restoration (whatever that looks like to you), patiently waiting for you to reach out and receive it.

People come into the room where you and Him are standing, but you're too overwhelmed with His beauty and kindness to care about what anyone else thinks.

As you reach out to receive restoration, not knowing what will happen, the scene changes and you're safe in His arms. You finally grasp His love for you. He says it's time to rest, to stay in that place, so you begin breathing slowly, soon deeply. You've never felt so calm. With eyes full of tears you ask, "Why me? Why do you love *me*?" Wrestling with the why, you think through your past, searching for a reason… but there is none. Then His eyes say what your heart has always longed to hear, "Beloved, I love you because it's *who I am.*"

As a prayer of thanksgiving, jot down a few words of how you're feeling in the space below:

—

It's easy to accept the lie that holding onto brokenness is our only option. The enemy screams at us that we're self sufficient, yet total failures. An illogical, yet somehow attractive statement. He lies to us, saying we don't need healing or we're beyond the point where it would make any difference anyway. He tries to convince us God is a band-aid and His love is a hippie joke… but that couldn't be further from the truth. His love is the bliss we long for.

As we learn to stay in that safe place with Him, fixing our eyes on Jesus, our wrong thoughts will be dismantled and we'll begin hearing new ones, the right ones. Often they can sound too good to be true, but that's the point. God is everything good we wish could be true. God is who He says He is. His love is sweet and you can trust Him.

One last thought to set the tone of this book, a core understanding that everything else here is built on.

Catherine, a friend of mine that's taught me a ton about life with God, uses a simple illustration to describe our relational position, or standing, with Him. She faces two chairs at one another explaining how when we think of God and us in this way, it can feel like we've been called into the Principal's office. But then she shares what the Scriptures say is true. That it more resembles the fact we're invited to sit in the middle of three chairs around us. In each one, God sits. Father, Son, and Holy Spirit. In that safe place we're surrounded by Love.[6] He's our protector, provider, advocate, and deepest friend. He's not against us, and we're not in trouble as He devises up a punishment to teach us a lesson. We're not there because of something we did wrong, and we don't have to make a case for why He should listen to us. We're literately *in God*.

Or, *in Love*.

It's here where every situation, whether big or small is seen and addressed by Him. Every part of life finds value regardless of circumstance or our assumptions: "For in Him we live and move and have our being." Acts 17v28a

The Father, Son, and Holy Spirit are often referred to as *the Trinity*. And what I can't get enough of, is that the Greek word for Trinity (περιχώρησις, or perikhōrēsis) means "rotation" or "divine dance." We're literally invited *into* God, into the divine dance of glory and enjoyment!

This was the relational intention, or blessing, in Genesis and it's again available to us because of Jesus in Holy Spirit.

So the invitation is open. This is the place we're after, God's love.

Jude, in his one page letter, says, "Keep yourselves in God's love…" (1v21). So as you find that place, stay there. That's where you're intended to live from. Constantly aware that you're safe in God.

I know it may be a simple analogy, but think of a balloon. It's fairly useless when deflated, but when filled with air, it takes full form. It's operating in its potential, and far more fun to play with. That's us. We choose what to be filled with. But like air to a balloon, Holy Spirit is the only one who can activate everything we're created to be.

So if this is true, then why is it so difficult to really believe it?

Good question. Let's start there.

Part One: Live

If there is a supreme creator God from whom everything came, then there's intention behind everything that exists. What then, is the intention behind living?

Is the point simply breathing in and out until we no longer can? Is it eating? Or drinking? Could it be working? How about chasing the feeling of accomplishment? Or having great sex? Is it all about accumulating what's viewed as valuable at any given moment in a society?

What if the unseen is just as valuable in the economy of intention as what's visible? What if the very thoughts we welcome have as much substance and worth as the movements we make? And what if those unseen thoughts are the starting line for everything we do? In this kind of economy, I believe our thoughts lead us internally to the ways we later express externally.

Simply put, what we think matters. And during our process of uncovering what life with God and each other can look like, both *what* and *how* we think matters just as much as the way we go about it in our actions, rhythms, and traditions. It's a fancy way of saying we gotta get the heart stuff right before we can attempt to work on the head stuff... or the hands stuff. Jesus talks about this in what's become known as *The Sermon on the Mount* in Matthew 5-7.

Every action we make is based off of what we're believing in that moment to be most true.

I drank a cup of coffee from my favorite shop this morning because I was convinced it was coffee and not poison. I thought, therefore I acted. This is why I suggest we start by working through what we *think* about God and ourselves in Part One, then move on to some practical stuff in Part Two.

"For in Him we *live* and move and have our being." Acts 17v28a

Welcome to Part One... Live.

What Happened?

Every story has a setting: the place, or type of surroundings, where something is positioned. Locale, time in space, the year or day, the mood and atmosphere, climate and geography, social and political and cultural environments, etc. These kinds of things surround everything we know, giving us points of reference.

When we think of skiing, snowy mountains may come to mind. When we think Portland, we may picture "Oregon." Everything sits somewhere and within something. Or we could say it this way, everything finds itself inside of a bigger a story. This is true for you and I as well. And while it seems easy enough to grasp, it leads to a really important question.

When we think of *God*, what is *His* setting?

And if *all of life* is *in God*, do I believe *I'm* a part of *His setting*? Do God and I overlap, or is there "God space" and then "my world," and they just happen to bump into each other sometimes?

In order to get our thoughts arranged, let's go back a few thousand, or million, or billion years[7] to look at His setting in which all this, creation, started. We'll use the Scriptures as our text.

In the beginning, or the genesis of all things, we see a Creator, creating.[8] This Creator builds a literal, physical world from an unseen one. Then at the apex of this glorious project, He[9] (I'd suggest reading this endnote) reveals and launches the original outline for humanity. Thus, people are sewn *into* the story, or fabric, of God. He shows them the world He's created, then…

We'll need to stop there for a minute. There's something really important to zoom in on at this point.

Genesis chapter one and two are basically the same story being told from two different camera angles. In some ways, that's what the first two chapters of the Bible are. Two tellings of the same story.[10]

Genesis 2v7 is the moment when the Creator shifts from making the world[11] to making people.

"Then the Lord God formed a man from the dust of the ground and breathed into his nostrils the breath of life, and the man became a living being."

After forming the physical body of this man, did you notice what the Creator did? He breathed *life* into him, and it was in that moment the man became a *living being*.

The Creator's first interaction with humanity was *giving* breath, or *life*.

While identity goes deeper than actions, our actions help identify what's happening on the inside. You wouldn't (hopefully) punch someone in the face for no reason. Something within you moved you to act on the feeling. In the same way, the Creator's first action with people, the first thing that came from who He is, was *life*. All life is from God. He is the originator and source of life, and as we'll discover, He can't *not be* life. Which is to say, He was life then (at the beginning), and He's still life now.

For us today, this means there's hope in colorless and dead situations that you find yourself in. It may be a relationship, finances, a work or school thing, but whatever it is, He's the life and color for those moments. A major part of the conversation in this book is learning and practicing how to let Him be Him for us.

Okay, so God's first interaction is giving breath, or life. Now check out what the other angle on the story reveals: His first *words* to humanity.

"God *blessed* them and said to them, "Be fruitful and increase in number; fill the earth and subdue it. Rule over the fish in the sea and the birds in the sky and over every living creature that moves on the ground." Genesis 1v28

His first relational action toward humanity was to *bless*.

So life and blessing comes from God.

Now, I'm not sure about you, but the word *blessing,* or *blessed,* has some major baggage attached. Even still, there's something helpful in the concept of *blessing* we don't want to miss. So what does "blessed" mean?

I saw a Range Rover all done up the other day with the license plate "BLESSD." *So you're telling me God blessed them with that?*

Maybe… actually yeah, He may have. I think it's best to refuse to live in a world of having to sort out and categorize everything God does. But the issue here comes when we think *blessing* is a purely physical and measurable *something*. Why is this dangerous? Because in that world, life becomes a game of comparison with a structure where we decide who is most *blessed*. But that's not helpful, and it's not the point. If anything, it distracts us from the One whom all blessing comes from anyways.

So for the sake of better understanding what happened at this moment in the story, the *blessing* part, let's use another word and phrase that may better line up with our context today while still maintaining the integrity of what the author was communicating:

Adoration and *deep love.*

So the first interaction the Creator has with humanity is giving life. And then the first relational moment He has with them is showing His *adoration* and *deep love* for them.

Sadly, many people don't see God this way. Maybe you do, or maybe you don't. It's a common conversation for people to read the Scriptures and get stuck on the effects of what takes place when we turn our face away from God's. Or in Bible words, the effects of sin.

But what if *life*, *adoration*, and *deep love* is who God wants to be for you? What good reason, outside our misunderstandings, could we have to reject His presence with us?

Take a minute to read the following lines and watch for the relational parts where we get a glimpse of His love for us:

"You see, at just the right time, when we were still powerless, Christ died for the ungodly. Very rarely will anyone die for a righteous person, though for a good person someone might possibly dare to die. But God demonstrates his own love for us in this: While we were still sinners, Christ died for us." Romans 5v6-8

"For those who are led by the Spirit of God are the children of God. The Spirit you received does not make you slaves, so that you live in fear again; rather, the Spirit you received brought about your adoption to sonship. And by him we cry, "Abba, Father." The Spirit himself testifies with our spirit that we are God's children." Romans 8v14-16

"But when the set time had fully come, God sent his Son, born of a woman, born under the law, to redeem those under the law, that we might receive adoption to sonship. Because you are his sons, God sent the Spirit of his Son into our hearts, the Spirit who calls out, "Abba, Father." So you are no longer a slave, but God's child; and since you are his child, God has made you also an heir." Galatians 4v4-7

"For he has rescued us from the dominion of darkness and brought us into the kingdom of the Son he loves, in whom we have redemption, the forgiveness of sins." Colossians 1v13-14

"Therefore, as God's chosen people, holy and dearly loved, clothe yourselves with compassion, kindness, humility, gentleness and patience." Colossians 3v12

Saved. Adopted. Now children of His. Redeemed. Freed. Brought close and given an inheritance. Rescued. Forgiven. Chosen. Loved. Oh, the childlike simplicity of Love.

May we grow in receiving the uncomplicated truths of *God for us* and *God with us.*

Let's practice.

—

Rhythm of Practicing Peace

Try this five times, spending five seconds on each step.

- Breathe in slowly
- Hold your breathing
- Breathe out

Now, five times spending seven seconds on each step.

- Breathe in slowly
  Hold your breathing
- Breathe out

Finally, five times spending twelve seconds on each step.

- Breathe in slowly
- Hold your breathing
- Breathe out

Pray: Jesus, thank you for Your deep love for me. Thank you that every breath I take in is from You, and every exhale leads me back to You. Even now, I'm reminded of how good You are to me.

This first chapter is based on the question, "What happened?" in reference to why the world is the way it is as addressed through the Scriptures. We've established the setting and looked briefly at two specific moments (life and blessing, from God, to humanity), but as we continue the Genesis scene changes and we're introduced to two more characters. A second person and a talking snake. Quick side note, whether this was literal or figurative, the concept stays the same. Careful not to get caught up on the talking snake bit, you'll miss what's going on. Be okay with wonder. It's a gift, not a curse.

"Now the serpent was more crafty than any of the wild animals the Lord God had made. He said to the woman, "Did God really say, 'You must not eat from any tree in the garden?'" The woman said to the serpent, "We may eat fruit from the trees in the garden, but God did say, 'You must not eat fruit from the tree that is in the middle of the garden, and you must not touch it, or you will die.'" "You will not certainly die," the serpent said to the woman. "For God knows that when you eat from it your eyes will be opened, and you will be like God, knowing good and evil." Genesis 3v1-5

Notice what the snake, that is Satan,[12] says to the woman… "Did God *really* say?"

This question is dripping with opposition against what their Creator had previously told them. A sneering, passive aggressive… "Don't *you* see what's *really* going on here" kind of tone.

This is how the enemy operates. Passive aggressive demoralization.

When God showed His affection and deep love toward humanity, it created identity in them. It established who they were, giving them an account to draw from when they felt empty and a basis for their understanding and existence for all of life. It was their safe place, without insecurity, where they were intended to stay as they enjoyed life, but God's adversary (and now ours too)[13] knew their identity was *the* primary element to attack.

Why was *identity* their weak spot? And why was exploiting it a brilliant strategy of the one who wanted to ruin them? Well, for one, the enemy knew if these people entertained *his* thoughts (lies) about who they were that everything would spiral into confusion. And when two opposing worlds collide, it gets messy quickly. I'd argue this is one of the most common reasons *life with God* can seem so difficult.

Confusion.

Our ability to fully function holistically is crippled when the very core of what we know about God and ourselves is challenged. Our confusion is the enemy's playground.

If the story stopped here, it'd prove to be a discouraging one, but God is all about healing, resetting, and reestablishing our messy thoughts about who He is. And from there, we come to know who we are. He longs for us to give Him the canvas of our attention, our assumptions, and our insecurities so that He can again paint an extravagant and colorful mural of who He is for us and who we are in Him.

God spoke specific blessing, putting on full display His adoration and deep love for these garden people, which in turn created a relational environment of safety and trust between them and Himself. This was the true state of bliss that God intended for us. To be surrounded by His holy presence.

That story is our story, and it raises the question, "What do I turn to for feelings of safety and trust?" Our response can be a helpful indicator of what we believe about God and ourselves at any given moment.

These people were safe in God, that's where their identity originated, and it was very good. Then the perfect setup broke because they allowed the source of their identity to be changed from Life to death. So where does your identity flow from?

Take a minute to make a short list of what you *give* your time to in a normal day:

Add a few things you constantly find yourself *thinking* about:

Now add what you *do* when you're stressed or worried:

Finally, write down people, rhythms, or actions (regardless if they're helpful/good or not) you find yourself running to when you need a break from the chaos of not being able to control everything. Movies, exercise, food, shopping, pornography, etc:

The goal here isn't to count all the off things we do and think. Rather, we're seeking to identify the lies that lead us to believe those habits are actually *better* than God's available localized presence (Holy Spirit).

Your list may help reveal where you tend to derive your identity. For me, I realized how much time I spend worrying about what others may think about me and my work. This leads to stressing over a number of things I do… thus it's easy for me to slip into an obsessive compulsive perfectionistic mindset and lifestyle. The lie being: If I'm not the best at what I do (validated by gaining people's approval), then I have no value. And for me, this helped a ton because it showed part of what's happening when I shift into that mindset. I now recognize the system when it's in front of me and am reminded it's broken. In turn, the next time I find myself wanting to launch into this cycle, I know to immediately shift my attention back to God and say, "God, I need you to reestablish my mind right now. I care more about what You think than what others think. Here I am, your son is listening."

He sees what you wrote down and the ones you didn't... but it doesn't change His adoration and deep love for you. There is no shame in His presence, rather, because of receiving His love in Jesus, you're actually *honored* in His presence.

If you choose to make this way of thinking a normal part of life, I bet you'll enjoy life with God more. I say this because He daily restructures the wrong ideas I hold of myself and others, replacing them with the truth. His thoughts.

So, the enemy questions what God says about us, then questions who God is to us.

In the Genesis story, right after raising the question about Eve's identity, the enemy moves onto questioning who God is to her. He says, "You will not certainly die," something their Creator did tell them *would* happen: "But you must not eat from the tree of the knowledge of good and evil, for when you eat from it you will certainly die." Genesis 2v17

What's going on here?

Humanity was given life and breath from God. They were blessed... adored, and deeply loved. All that, coming from their Creator resulted in an obvious ease of trusting He was who He said He was. In fact their relationship with Him was close and not distant, so much that Genesis 3v8 says, "Then the man and his wife heard the sound of the Lord God as he was walking in the garden in the cool of the day..."

They literally got to walk with God... *wow.*

And now the enemy moved into questioning what Eve knew to be true, first by messing with her identity, then with the way she related to her identity source.

I'd dare to say our world isn't broken because of the enemy's power as much as because we listen to him. What we think about God and ourselves shapes how we live.

And unfortunately Eve chose to believe the enemy's lies over what her Creator said.

Notice… she heard what the enemy said, but the universe was still right. It was the moment she (and then the man as well) *received* what the enemy said that everything broke. In essence, she copied and pasted lies directly in place of God's words for her life. Words of life, blessing, and deep love were exchanged for ones of skepticism, suspicion, and confusion.

Life was not programed to thrive, much less exist, alongside confusion. The enemy knew that, and God knew that, but who humanity chose to believe was up to them. Love trusts. It leaves room.[14]

But even in this moment, the one we find ourself in, God's grace and love is made known by His ongoing invitation for us to return to Him.[15]

So, that's what happened…

Everything in the Scriptures is intended to be chewable. I don't believe its primary intention is a record book, but a workout book, showing us what God is like over and over and over… especially in the face of our rebellion.

This story, among other things, leads us to ask what lies we've chosen to believe. Where have we listened to the enemy, pasting his lies over the truth our Creator has spoken to us? We'll talk a bit more about this later on in a chapter called *Learning to Trust*.

Thankfully the garden story isn't over.

Yes, relationship is now broken.

Yes, trust has been twisted into a confusing and messy relational knot of tension.

And yes, humanity listens to the one who wants hell for them.[16] Not a great moment in history, but God is all about restoration. He wants His family back and is going to fight for it. More specifically, He's willing to let Himself be treated the way we deserve so that we can be treated the way He deserves. This is what God is like.

—

Rhythm of Practicing Peace

Prayer: Father, thank you. Thank you for how good You are to me. Thank you for never giving up on me. Thank you for always calling me home. Thank you for loving me when I choose to be unlovable. Thank you for calling me *Your Beloved*.

If all this is true, then I want healing too. I say yes to who You want to be for me. Thank you for making it possible to be close to You again. Come be everything for me You want to be, I give up control and am choosing to follow You today.

—

The story is only beginning to unfold as more people enter the scene. Some want to know their Creator, while others put their efforts into making a name for themselves. The effects of choosing to live in confusion play out as the majority world continues fighting for control, causing even more chaos and pain amidst the scattered beauty. But God knows, His heart longs for humanity to walk with Him, in Him, again.

And eventually, this is what Jesus comes to restore: relationship between us and Him, us and each other, and us and all of creation.

I can't wait for you to get to the next chapter. It's where all this is leading. But before we continue, here's something to think about.

What if your greatest challenge isn't the enemy, but believing what God says about you?[17]

Because stories often help to transfer the understanding behind words better than simply stating the point, here's another way to think of it. Another way to grasp this idea.

There was a young boy sitting at the school lunch table when a bully walked up and sat down next to him. The bully said, "You're ugly. I don't like you," then walked away. The boy began to cry because it hurt, a lot. He didn't know how to process what had happened and began believing what he'd just heard.

That afternoon as he got off the bus, his parents could see his deep sadness, hurt, and confusion in his eyes, posture, and dampened tone.

As he walked into the living room with his head low, tears welling up, his parents said, "Son, come sit up on the sofa with us" so the boy climbed up into his parent's laps and for a few moments he was content just being held. Crying, but loved.

After some time had passed, they lifted his chin, looked in his eyes and said, "Did you know, you're the most handsome boy we've ever seen? The way you comb your hair, and your eyes, oh your eyes! We love your eyes! We like your fingers, and your toes, and your nose. We're so glad you're our boy. There's nothing in the world that can make us stop loving you. You're becoming everything you're intended to be, and we love you because we love you because we love you."

Of course the boy stayed in those arms for hours. He didn't want to leave. And eventually he fell asleep.

The next morning his parents said it all over again, reminding him how much they loved him and what they see when they look at him.

The boy stood up a little straighter as a tender smile broke across his face. He no longer had anything to prove. He felt full, safe, secure, and wanted.

The day went on, and now at school, the lunch bell rang. As he sat down to eat, the bully bumped his way past the other kids and forced himself into the seat next to the boy. But this time was different. When the bully started his attack, "You're ugly and I don't...," the boy interrupted him before he could finish, and quoted word for word what his parents had said about him.

The bully stood up and left because he realized he no longer had authority or power of control through fear, shame, and guilt. This little boy knew who he was again.

You see, I'm convinced our greatest challenge isn't the enemy, but believing what God says about us. And in that place the enemy has little power and zero authority. You are made in God's image, and He's never for a moment turned His face of delight from you.

I love what my friend Brandon says, "God is in a good mood, just waiting for us to join in on the conversation."

—

Rhythm of Practicing Peace

As you set things aside, ask: "Father, thank you for being here with me right now. What are Your thoughts about me?"

Jot down what you feel He may be saying to you, then share what you hear with a friend.

Moving From god to Abba

As you read the next few pages, my prayer for you is similar to one I ask most days:

Father, open our eyes to know You're with us right now. May we recognize and receive Your invitation to move from thinking about You as a far off, distant, and impersonal god to a close, connected, and knowable one... our Abba.

Teach us to quiet ourselves so that we can listen... ready for conversation with You. Activate our entire being to connect with You in every way possible.

Show us what's corrupted in our thinking and life and give us a desire for you to replace it with whatever is true. We long to speak with You face to face like a friend, knowing Your kindness toward us.

Now, in whatever way makes sense for you, tell Him how you're feeling. Tell Him about the way you wish you could know Him. About who you long for Him to be for you. He loves when we ask.

—

If you were asked to point to God.. what would your default reaction be?

Would you point *up*?

Most people do, not everyone, but most.

Why is that?

Why is it so natural to assume God is… *up*?

While we could trace back through history to where this idea began, that's not what we're after. Rather, I want us to wrestle with the effect that this thought (thinking God is *up)* has on us in relation to grasping the expansive revelation that we're designed to closely and intimately do life with God 24/7. An all the time, give and take relationship, just like breathing.[18]

But before we dive in, we need to consider a foundational concept: the analogy and reality of *God as our Father*.

It's pretty normal in our culture for young people to grow up with divorce some where in their direct family. And while divorce doesn't define whether parents are "good" or "bad," something does happen deep in the nucleus of a family when Dad and Mom pull apart outwardly.

Because of these broken parental experiences, some will argue that the *God as Father* picture doesn't work anymore. The argument says it's no longer a relationship that most can draw meaning from. To which I'd raise the question… if that's the case, are we basing our relational understanding of God off of a broken form we see in the world rather than allowing Him to create the grid we use to see the world? In other words, even in a great family (the kind everyone wishes they could be a part of), those parents aren't God. Therefore, to base our understanding of God off of them is to define God by them. And personally, that scares me. A lot. It means we're attempting to put a human identity ceiling on a supernatural God.[19]

This is part of what I want us to think about.

How much of God are you accessing? Not in a percentage amount, but a relational one.

Or here's another way to think about it... a Facebook *friend* can be very different than someone you spend time with physically. In the same way it's possible to call God, "God," but only know Him like you do a Facebook friend, "god." Limited access.

There's a massive opportunity for *knowing about* to become *truly knowing.*

My desire is to take a journey together in hopes of exploring what it could look like to move from relating to (what may feel like) a far off god that you sing to on Sunday, and enter into a place of *knowing* that He's close and invites you to call Him "Abba" (Papa, Father, Daddy).

It's there where you can finally rest because you begin to receive the truth that you're His beloved, His child. It's roomy and there's plenty of space to *enjoy* life with God and others in that place.

For some, you've been here before and turned around.

For others you're longing to know your heavenly Father like this.

And for others, this will be the last line you'll read before setting this book down.

That's okay.

In various ways, some of this may be uncomfortable. It's possibly a reframing of years and years of thinking. It may feel like a restructuring of what you've been taught since you were young. For others, it may seem like you already know this, but to think we have it figured out leaves no room for God to teach us. I'd encourage you to stay open to Holy Spirit as you read.

Whatever it is for you, I hope it's more of a growth in paradigm than a tossing out of an old system.

Our Father isn't scared of the wrong systems of thought and broken ideas we hold. In fact He longs to heal them for us, patiently whispering to His children who have run away and found themselves lost, hurting, and confused.[20]

He longs for us to come home. To return to delight.

So as we let Him speak, learning to listen to His voice (especially in ways that may be unfamiliar), I think we'll experience what it's like to move from feeling distant to close.

For some of us, rules are the easy part, but letting someone love us... well that's the hard part. Pride, in whatever form it takes, is a relational drug habit of individualism that we gotta drop if we want to move forward.

Learning to let Him love us will start the process of dissolving the tangled, blurry, and hopeless thought of God being *up* and *far away*, ruling this planet from some clouded, locked, and oppressive throne.

The revelation that He's local, closer than your own breath, must replace the illusion of a far off, unknowable, and emotionally distant *god*.

He longs for us to experience Him as our perfect Father. For us to become as wrapped up in Him as a newborn is with her mother. Her life depends on her mom yes, but she also finds her safe, hiding, and secure place being held closely against the One who gave her life. And He, like a mother, is deeply in love with us not because of anything we've done, but because of who He is for us: "We love because *He first loved us*." 1 John 4v19.

Calling God a certain name isn't the goal here. It's learning to cultivate a heart posture of receiving His love. One where we let Him in. One where every door in the house of our lives is open for Him to come in and move stuff around. He won't impose Himself on us. He always waits for us to take His hand. This posture is central to grasping and living in our God-adopted reality designed for all eternity.

May we move from thinking about God as "god," to knowing our Abba as He longs to be known.

—

Rhythm of Practicing Peace

Read the following verses slowly, picturing in your mind's eye what God is saying to you:

"The Spirit you received does not make you slaves, so that you live in fear again; rather, the Spirit you received brought about your adoption to sonship. And by him we cry, "Abba, Father." The Spirit himself testifies with our spirit that we are God's children." Romans 8v15-16

"But when the time had fully come, God sent his Son, born of a woman, born under law, to redeem those under law, that we might receive the full rights of sons. Because you are sons, God sent the Spirit of his Son into our hearts, the Spirit who calls out, "Abba, Father." So you are no longer a slave, but a son; and since you are a son, God has made you also an heir." Galatians 4v4-7

The words "son" and "sonship" were contextual to their society. They mean *children*, which unequivocally includes *daughters*. For this reason, let's read the verses again, but this time in The Message translation which, in my opinion, is a better expression of what the text is saying:

"This resurrection life you received from God is not a timid, grave-tending life. It's adventurously expectant, greeting God with a childlike "What's next, Papa?" God's Spirit touches our spirits and confirms who we really are. We know who he is, and we know who we are: Father and children." Romans 8v15-16

"But when the time arrived that was set by God the Father, God sent his Son, born among us of a woman, born under the conditions of the law so that he might redeem those of us who have been kidnapped by the law. Thus we have been set free to experience our rightful heritage. You can tell for sure that you are now fully adopted as his own children because God sent the Spirit of his Son into our lives crying out, "Papa! Father!" Doesn't that privilege of intimate conversation with God make it plain that you are not a slave, but a child? And if you are a child, you're also an heir, with complete access to the inheritance." Galatians 4v4-7

If you've never used words like "Abba," "Daddy," "Papa," or "Father" (in a relational, not *because you're supposed to* kind of way) to interact with God, as a child of God, I'd encourage you to try it now. It may be a simple prayer, or it may be a long one, but the names we use to start a conversation often set the trajectory for what kind of conversation we're about to have. And the beauty is that He invites us to start every conversation with Him from this place.

Try starting a conversation with Him now as a child talks to her father. Nothing more, nothing less. Be patient as you listen for Him to respond, then write down what you feel He might be saying to you:

Relationship to Worship

This chapter is a bit longer so I've broken it into a few sections: *The Introduction, The Ugly Rock, and What Does The Word "Worship" Mean?*

The Introduction

As the desire to know Him in fresh ways builds inside of you… I'm guessing something *will* happen. You'll notice a shift in your thinking and decisions. You'll no longer view them through a lens of shame and guilt constantly using the system of *is this good, or this is bad* (with the experience of emotion to follow.) Instead you'll find yourself in an ongoing, unending conversation with Him where you're safe, loved, and aware of His leading. This is what I mean by *moving from god to Abba.*

The movement of learning to know Him as near and as the One who delights in you, your Abba, can change everything. From here, another form of relationship begins to grow. We actually become *worshipers* of God. A people who reflect, in expression, the deep love and adoration of our Father, Jesus, and Holy Spirit back to God.

Our attention intentionally directed.

Our whole being seeking to love God.

Becoming a God worshiper is simply turning our face towards His to adore Him once again. And in doing so, handing everything we've begun thinking is ours to control… back to Him.

This term *worshipers* is used a few times in the Scriptures to refer to His family. And while today it usually lands in religious contexts, it's simply referring to the idea of *serving*. Serving something or someone can be out of commitment, sure, or it can come from a constant affection and adoration of that thing or person.

He knows we're shaped by what we give ourselves to so He invites us into living a life of worship directed towards Him. He unapologetically wants to bless us by giving all of who He is.

Try thinking about it this way… the person who consistently works out at the gym, like my buddy Brad, will look a certain way because of it. He's by far the strongest guy I know!

The person who reads all day long… guess what their topic of conversation will float around?

Or the person who skateboards, or listens to music, or plays a sport… and on and on we could go.

So in other words, we express outwardly what we've accepted inwardly. What we surround ourselves with has a massive impact on who we become.

Some ask how Jesus was constantly with people "far from God" and yet wasn't drawn into their mindsets or led to act like them. I'd argue it was because He knew and practiced what it meant to live *in God*. Jesus was God, yes, but in being human He got to cultivate the art of unending conversational exchange with His Abba. And as a Jesus follower and disciple, He's given us everything we need to know about how to start the process. Because of Holy Spirit, we have the same access to the Father as Jesus did! We too can choose to live in an atmosphere of an unending conversational exchange with our Abba.

As we learn to enjoy our Creator for who He says He is to us, a process will take place leaving us different than the moment before. And it's because He knows we become like what we worship that He longs for us to see His kindness, to be moved to repentance (meaning to turn around, or return home),[21] and to enjoy the most full life accessible in Him.

Getting to know Him as your Abba and living a life of worship go hand in hand.

So what does moving from relationship to worship look like in our day to day? Well, I'd suggest it starts with how we think about the concept of *worship*. Similarly to the idea of *moving from god to Abba*, the move is not about abandoning the former to achieve the latter. Rather, it's an evolution and push into your next stage of doing life with God. Some call this *going deeper* like the picture we see in The Message translation of Ephesians 3v16-19:

"I ask him to strengthen you by his Spirit – not a brute strength but a glorious inner strength – that Christ will live in you as you open the door and invite him in. And I ask him that with both feet planted firmly on love, you'll be able to take in with all Christians the extravagant dimensions of Christ's love. Reach out and experience the breadth! Test its length! Plumb the depths! Rise to the heights! Live full lives, full in the fullness of God."

Personally, I like that way of thinking about it. As we continually return to Him,[22] He takes delight in us, and our capacity to experience more who He is expands because we're in a place of being willing to receive. And by receiving Him into every second and breath, He becomes our God, our Lord. It's in this place, an on-going life of worshiping our Abba, we can find the truest fulfillment in life.

If we picture our minds like a construction site, we need to clear the debris so that we can lay a solid foundation for the way we think and live. One piece of debris we need to remove is called *moralistic therapeutic deism*, an idea that's commonly accepted in Western Christianity and extremely destructive to our relationship with God.

Sociologists Christian Smith and Melinda Lundquist Denton first used this term in their book, *Soul Searching: The Religious and Spiritual Lives of American Teenagers,* noting five beliefs of the dominant religion of contemporary American teenagers.

They are:

"A God exists who created and orders the world and watches over human life on earth. God wants people to be good, nice, and fair to each other, as taught in the Bible and by most world religions. The central goal of life is to be happy and to feel good about one-self. God does not need to be particularly involved in one's life except when he is needed to resolve a problem." And, "Good people go to heaven when they die."

In other words: God wants you to be nice, do good things, and feel good about yourself. That's it.

Nothing about interaction or blissful relationship with God.

To subscribe to this way of thinking makes God seem like an absent father who sends an annual birthday card rather than the one who is constantly present... and it's just not true.

This extremely limited view of the Christian faith can stand like a dam between a desert and a deep lake where God is inviting us to swim.

The Ugly Rock

Have you ever gotten an idea stuck in your head and because of it, acted differently than you would have without it?

Here's what I mean... imagine being convinced a friend is upset with you, but they won't tell you why. How does this change the way you'll act the next time you're around them? Chances are you may be quietly defensive or outright critical because of the assumptions you're living by.

Or how about being convinced you're going to fail a test? Each response is marked with timidity and a sort of dread for your final score to be revealed. Why? Because your entire being is engaged with this idea of failure… and we act based upon what we think is true.

So whatever the idea, whether helpful or not, good or bad, one reality remains the same about all of them. Ideas are *really* powerful.

Think about the movie Inception. If you haven't seen it yet, rent it tonight (and while you're at it, rent Interstellar too). It's a brilliant story about the influence an idea can have on a person, and the weight it carries in determining ones future decisions.

Point is, what we think matters.

But here's what's crazy… while we know the ideas we accept play a major part in shaping who we are, I'm not convinced we spend enough time sorting through the ones we're subscribed to. We live in a time where content and ideas are prostituted to whoever will listen or watch, and we're the audience. The one's caught in the crossfire of the vomit of attempted communication between companies, organizations, and individuals. And with that, we become hoarders of unfinished thoughts.

We consume all we want, but are left with a library of books we'll never fully read. We collect not for the sake of learning or growing as humans, but for the thrill of getting more… that momentary spark of excitement when one of our many screens reads, "Your order has been placed."

And somewhere in our overloaded minds, bursting with undeveloped and thoughtlessly accepted ideas is one idea that's quietly leading us toward a dry life with God. It's an idea we must dig out before we can move forward… let's call it *the ugly rock.*

Here it is… *"Worship is just something we do at church."*

That's it.

It's that simple. And yet, it has the potential to derail us from enjoying

Him in the most real, raw, and un-makeup-ed moments of our lives, the 99%.

But if we're honest, it's the unspoken assumption right?

Church, worship… work week… then *church* and *worship* again.

In a slightly exaggerated, yet unfortunately honest way, an all too common reality is to go the Sunday gathering[23] then head out the doors and attempt to "live by the rules" until next week. The songs we sing[24] alongside a ton of other people who we're convinced are far better at life with God than us, can offer the promise of feeling like we're in some Jesus club that gives us access to a blurry promise of "an afterlife not burning in hell" that the Pastor seems to grasp, but we nod like we get it so that we don't look dumb. And the sermon… if we can sit through that and take good notes, then we're quietly assured (though we'd never say it out loud) that we're all loaded up with something that will keep us "good" during the week. At least until that moment when our perception of failure happens, but then again… that may be why we go back. Oh, and maybe a quick prayer or two before dinner or during a sports game.

I know I said be careful in throwing away systems of thought earlier… but that one is worth throwing out.

The enemy uses *that* system, one of shame and guilt, anytime we choose to live in something other than an intimate relationship with God, our Abba.

But please hear my heart in this. All those practices… the Sunday gathering, the singing, and the teaching from the Scriptures, they're all good. In-fact they're *really* good, but unless they move us to *worship* God from the deep core of who we really are, then they're hollow at best.

There will be days where we have to make ourselves sing even when the words don't feel natural, while other times they express perfectly what we're feeling. I think both are okay, and only human, after all… life with God and each other isn't a formula, so it won't always work the way we want it to.

Simply put, *a life of worship* is the expression of life in God. To subdivide it as its own, once a week activity, is like trying to separate a living body and breathing…together, the rhythm they create is life itself. This is why *the ugly rock* issue exists, because most of our Western minds lustfully want boxes and boundaries to put everything in which results in religious systems, traditions, and practices for the sake of proof.

Worship is more than just singing. It's a mindset, a heart posture, and a lifestyle of constant re-directed attention, affection, wonder, and awe toward our Abba and His goodness seen in all of life.

A 24/7 life of worship changes the weekly gathering from a *have to* into a *get to.* It becomes a celebration with God's family and those looking in, curious about what it all means. It shifts the point of the teaching from information… to encountering. It becomes a party where hope in every situation in life is possible again because of Jesus' resurrection, no matter how badly we messed up. A moment where we're reminded about what's most true and where as a family, we get to celebrate *the glory of God who is with us* regardless of our failures. Our attention, both individually and communally, is drawn back and forward to the one that has taken us out of the kingdom of darkness and brought us into the kingdom of the Son He loves (Colossians 1v13).

With that said, the notion that "worship is just something we do at church" is only the tip of the iceberg, and unfortunately, an issue equally dangerous lies directly under the surface. An issue set against the very core of our lives with God.

Maybe there's a specific theologic term for it, but I simply call it *geographic relational dualism.*

It's a way of thinking that says God is somehow bound to a place, a building, or a certain time of the week. In this case Sundays (or whenever the community you're a part of gathers). And rather than the

24/7 relational conversational back and forth-ness intended for us, we put our "normal week" in one box and "singing about or to God"[25] in another.

God's greatest desire for you isn't that you'd constantly sing familiar mainstream "worship songs" all week… it's *so* much bigger than that. He's bigger than that. Those songs are like the frame of a house, but the foundation is your willingness and desire to want God.

It's the difference between knowing about, and actually knowing. The difference between something you've heard verses something you can teach. The difference between head and heart.

And while songs written with the intention of reminding us of who He is can help move us forward into that place again and again… they themselves are guides, not the goal. If *worship* is the journey, then awareness and adoration for Father, Son, and Holy Spirit is the destination.

Simply put, *a life of worship* isn't captured by traditional church songs filling your iPod. It may include them, but it's so much bigger than a systematic approach to checkbox religious standards. So then what *is* a life of worship?

Well, have you ever noticed it's difficult to grasp the grandness of something until you've been there or experienced it, but the moment you get to experience it you realize why others couldn't explain it well enough for you to grasp?

I think it's kind of like that.

A unique and extremely personal, yet corporate and communal way of living where you become constantly aware that your soul is literally connected to God and that all of who He is loves you. That revelation will mess you up in the best way possible. Letting yourself believe it changes everything.

I think it's similar to the way art can achieve such powerful expression. Words have multiple meanings, and even now you may be interpreting what I'm writing differently than I'd intended it. I may not be able to express to you what the color blue is without referencing a blue object, but I can paint a blue line on your hand and in an instant, the something behind the word *blue* is transferred. Art is a wonderful and full form of communication.

Life with God isn't intended to be a perfect formula. Some of it is difficult to explain because it's for you to *know and experience*, not just to read or learn about. I believe a life of worship rarely just happens, it's more often practiced, cultivated, and learned. Expressed in numerous ways, a life of worship is the ongoing celebration of the glory of God (in this case, referring to *His goodness* or *character*).

Jesus came to show both what God is like and what a life of worship looks like. The access made possible through His life, death, and resurrection is the same access that opens the door for us to move from knowing about God to being able to experience life with Him. This is our starting ground to living a life of worship, seeing how good God is.

In freedom, we don't need to know how every conversation with God is supposed to be organized. Honest, real, valuable relationship is unscripted. And so, life with God, and a life of worship will be messy at times (both your perception of it and how others may view you), but that's where the freedom is. Life with God should never feel like you're on the Truman show. I like what Judah Smith said years ago (paraphrased): "Life with God should feel like a comfy Ikea couch you can sink into, not like a formal dining room where you'll mess up the neatly vacuumed carpet lines."

God is for you, and in Him is total freedom. And a life of worship is constant awareness and reaction to His goodness.

I remember the first few months of being married, looking in the fridge for a snack only to find vegetables, chicken, and almond milk.

"Where's the good stuff?" I'd say to myself.

Up to this point in my life I'd lived on cereal, peanut butter, and macaroni. And while I knew what a healthy diet looked like, it was super difficult for me to buy food based on those principles because grocery stores stress me out and I'm a creature of rhythm and routine. I like what I'm used to… which isn't always a good thing. It had gotten me stuck. I'd found my rut and was comfortable there.

Cereal.

Milk.

Peanut butter.

Macaroni.

The problem was I didn't always feel energized. But it was funny how over that first year of marriage healthy food became my new normal. There was no need to muster up the self control for *a week of healthy meals*, rather it became an all the time thing. It was in that place, for the first time in my adult life, I began to truly enjoy the tastes, textures, and the art of a good meal.

What's the point?

The point is, until we grasp and experience a life of *all the time worship*, we're missing out and may not even realize it.

For some, it may feel unfamiliar at first to intentionally worship God in your everyday moments, most of which are outside of a formal church gathering. But it has a really simple start… changing the way we think about life with God. A life of worship is not only possible, it's what you and I were created for. But if we refuse to release the idea that worship is just something we do at church on Sundays, it's going to be frustrating, uncomfortable, and outright confusing to try and make the move into a *worship is like breathing* way of life.

I'd forgotten that food was intended to be enjoyed, not just consumed. I was on auto-pilot when it came to eating. Eat to charge up for the day, but that's it. Only after being reminded of its beauty did I realized how limited my view had been. A whole new level of experiencing life happened for me in those months. It became far less about me trying to enjoy food, and way more about letting food be what it was intended to be for me. This simple reminder changed my entire life.

And just like that, I think we're supposed to remind each other God actually *wants us to enjoy Him*.

That said, as you work through these next few thoughts, remember they're built on the reality that worship isn't just *something we do*, as much as a constant and natural outflow of *who we are*. Worship flows from the heart. It's both a discipline and an art. A sacrifice and a receiving.

It's less about an act (lifting your hands, etc.) and more about choosing to be aware of who He is. This awareness leads us towards an outward response.

If you like pictures, or they help you learn, think about *breathing*. It's an unsolicited and often ignored rhythm of life. It's normal. A life of worship is as simple, and can become as natural for you, as breathing. And great news... you're already good at it! Each moment, you're inhaling and exhaling thoughts and feelings, assigning value to the things around you. You have daily patterns, things you find yourself doing simply because you've done them before. Some are helpful, others are destructive, but know this... new patterns are possible. Old ones can be done away with. Jesus longs to heal our whole self, and as we learn to live from a place of remembering that we're in God, constantly aware of Daddy's love and nearness... fear, shame, and guilt will no longer be our language of operation, rather love.

Finding a new normal can be something we're forced into because of a traumatic event, but there are also moments when we can choose to move forward into foreign places of new normals being established. I hope this is the start, or furthering, of one of those moments for you and God.

As we continue to explore what it could look like to move from relationship into worship, may the healthiest, most full and life giving truths and realities of Jesus bring about a new normal in you. One of inhaling love and exhaling worship.

"I bless God every chance I get; my lungs expand with his praise. I live and breathe God" Psalm 34v1-2a (The Message)

May peace, joy, and grace be yours in abundance.

—

Rhythm of Practicing Peace

Spend your next few minutes breathing in and out slowly. Ask Holy Spirit to calm your thoughts, settle your worries, and establish a sound mind in you as you meditate on who He is.

While you read the following verse, imagine being in the situation the writer is explaining. Being trapped in a dark room with no way to escape. Picture His hand reaching to save you and as He lifts you up into a spacious place, a well lit place. Then ask Him *why* He's saving you.

"I, the LORD, have called you in righteousness; I will take hold of your hand. I will keep you and will make you to be a covenant for the people and a light for the Gentiles, to open eyes that are blind, to free captives from prison and to release from the dungeon those who sit in darkness." Isaiah 42v6-7
He wants to set you free because He loves you. It's always because He loves you. And it will always be because He loves you.

Prayer: Thank you that You're everywhere all the time. That no moment exists where You've left me. Thank you that You see me right now and are here. That You know my heart, my thoughts, and my desires… and You still love me. Unwilling to leave me where I am, always breathing new life into me, always bringing me into new wonderful places. I want to cultivate a life of worshiping You in my everyday normal moments, one where I get to delight in You all the time. I want to know You the way You're inviting me to. Jesus, I want to be free to enjoy You more.

—

Sometimes we get to wait for His voice. I don't know why… but I do know it's worth the wait. It may cost you time and will surely require your attention and self-control. But His voice is kind, always whispering what's best because He loves you. And while it remains a mystery (or *within* mystery) why He relentlessly loves us, He simply loves us because it's who He is. He cannot operate out of any other reality, and it's who He longs to be for you.

As we live in awe, we're overhauled into the fullness of what it means to be human. We becoming a people who walk with our Abba again. A people who breathe His life back to Him.

This is what it means to live a life of worship in our everyday.

What Does The Word "Worship" Mean?

Rather than an exhaustive explanation, this next section is intended to offer a bit of clarity when we hear the word "worship."

In Isaiah 29v13, we see God's perspective of a situation involving worship. Probably a good place to start:

"The Lord says: "These people come near to me with their mouth and honor me with their lips, but their hearts are far from me. Their worship of me is made up only of rules taught by men.""

In other words, we can sing, lift our hands, get on our knees, lay on the floor, slip off our shoes, speak in tongues, wave flags, sing along to "worship music" (song created in hopes of leading people's attention and affection toward God), light candles, or whatever and totally not be "worshiping." All of which have the potential to be wonderful forms of expressing our awareness of His goodness, but no system or practice can *produce* worship.

Nor *is* any system worship.

Even when we're led into worship by these things, they in themselves are more like the art or path… but it's in our contemplation and response that we find the beginning of true worship happening. It's a heart thing. It has to be… otherwise we're working from a system, not a relationship.

Like any healthy, real, raw relationship, emotions are scattered along the journey. We experience these feelings when we perceive that we're being loved, accepted, seen, approved, valued, restored, released, set free, established, forgiven, and so on. From God, now a part of humanity, emotions are meant to enhance life. We're connected beings… mind, will, and emotions. All requiring balance and fine tuning by the One who made them.

When we're healthy, these different, yet connected parts of who we are *should* effect each other. These feelings that occur are a major part of what it means to be in the image and likeness of God, but be cautious when they become the measure of a "successful time of worship."

I made this mistake a few years ago.

In college, I had a playlist called, "soak." It was comprised of a handful of worship recordings from a few church communities I really enjoyed. These songs played through my headphones most days as I skated to class or work and evoked a certain emotional response in me. They played a part in creating an atmosphere of faith, which helped move me into a place of wanting to worship God. I think Paul and Silas may have experienced a similar thing as they sang in prison:

"About midnight Paul and Silas were praying and singing hymns to God, and the other prisoners were listening to them." Acts 16v25

I'm guessing one would sing and the other's perspective would shift, drafting the other into a heart of worship as well. That's what these songs were for me, a voice to lead me into that place with Him.

Years later I was playing these songs as background music with the assumption that they'd still move me… only to find they no longer did. It was in that moment I saw my value system of worship for what it had slowly become. It had been degraded to the point where the sweetest memories of delighting in God through these specific songs were nothing more than reliance on an emotional drug known as my "soak" playlist. I had reassigned the value given to me to give to Him, and was now assigning value to the melodies, lyrics, and memories I had with the songs themselves.

I experienced some great moments of honest worship through those songs. The problem was my heart posture. And heart posture is complex. It's messy, and gray, and nearly impossible to explain. But I believe it's in these moments that God's patience is clear as He parents us. He knows what's really going on inside… and still doesn't give up on us.

So if heart posture isn't always black and white, and worship flows from that place, then worship may not be something we're suppose to try and break down to a science either. Rhythms like song and the giving of our time, energy, and resources are wonderful (and I'd argue should be practiced by every Jesus follower), but can't guarantee to produce a heart of worship.

If you look up the definition of the word *worship* in an English dictionary you'll find it's not aimed at God by default.
Worship: "Reverent honor and homage paid to God or a sacred personage, or to any object regarded as sacred."

In other words, worship can be directed at nearly anything. We all do it. The worshiper gets to choose where they direct their attention. And while this limited and partial definition gives us directional insight into what worship is, there's so much more to understand.

When the God-fearing authors of the Hebrew Scriptures (the Old Testament) used this concept it meant something much more specific than just "honor and homage."[26] The word they often used to communicate this idea can be transliterated[27] *shachah* and means *to bow down*, or *return to the place we were created*.

Like we've established, worship is our response to who He is. And it's as we move from relating to Him as a far off god and step into the place of enjoying the full reality that He's inviting us to call Him Abba (my close and knowable God) that we can't help but bow down under the weight of who He is.

"Nate, are you saying I'm just going to fall on the ground randomly when I worship?"

Well, maybe. But more specifically, as you lean in to hear what He's saying, your entire self (mind, will, and emotions) is open to connect with what He says, and as His words water your soul it produces a living response. This can emerge as a song. At other times, speaking in tongues. Others will have a driving desire to paint, write, or create something beautiful in hopes to reflect or express what they're experiencing with their Abba. Others can't help but cry or laugh,[28] their emotional guards (or fear of what others may think) are let down in that moment.[29] And still other times we may feel the urge to slip off our shoes and lay on the ground because we're experiencing, and are aware of, what the Father told Moses was *holy ground*.

That's incredible. Holy ground… it exists. His very presence changes our surroundings. And the best part is, He's constantly inviting us to come into those spaces with Him. Set apartness, holiness, and sacredness (heaven on earth) on the physical substance called earth that you and I are standing on, and we can be aware of it! As His children, we have the authority to bring His rule and reign with us everywhere we go.

Oh that we'd ask Him to make us more aware of His nearness and love. He longs for us, in love, to take hold of the authority He's given us so that this world would know His bliss.

It's powerful to be reminded of who He really is and to become aware of His presence.[30] This is what leads to a full life.[31] And *a full life* is based in freedom because we're no longer bound under a ceiling of what *I'm* capable of or limited by, but we're set free into the unfathomable riches of who *He is*. Living *in Jesus* means your life is expanding all the time because you're searching and receiving the depths of who He is.

You may be behind on bills, but you can become so focused on the favor He has to answer your need that your attention becomes fixed on Him rather than the problem. When we live like this, problems are secondary and looking to Him for His blessing (starting and ending with His local presence) is primary.

We're His kids, not His paid workers, which means we can *always* go *directly* to Him. There's no line to wait in, or speech needed to convince Him why He should listen to us. Luke 15v11-32 is a perfect example. He's not looking down on us with a critical or angry brow. He loves you in the way you only dream possible.

So why have we adopted the, "God *if* you want to help me…" lifestyle? That's not a form found in heaven, therefore it's not one we have to subscribe to. Jesus set us free from that mentality and free from having to believe the lies that go along with it. We'll talk more about lies in a few chapters. They have no right to be in your life as a child of God except for the place you give them.

—

Rhythm of Practicing Peace

Pray out loud as if you were sitting side by side with Him:

Abba, I want to live free. I agree with what You say… that You're my close and loving Father and that Your way is best. I receive the freedom You want to give me in _____ (a situation you know it's needed).

However you're moved right now, in response to His love for you, do it. If it's repenting, go for it. If it's obeying what He's saying, now's the moment to say *yes*. His way is always the best and always leads to freedom.

—

This chapter is about *worship* and continues to circle back to *who He is*.

That's the point.

When we get that, worship happens. It'll be our response.

Of course, there will be times where we don't feel like expressing a life of worship in certain ways, but that's part of the process. While it can feel like we're "losing our faith," or "questioning everything we know," I'd suggest these moments of *choosing* to trust God is who He says He is can be the most beautiful ones. It takes a seed to be buried before it can grow. Our thinking to die before His can blossom in us.

Our emotions and excitement will not sustain a constant life of worship. They only play a part in enhancing it. Worship is a choice because it's established within a relationship of love… and love leaves room.

It's no coincidence the moments where we have to choose to worship can be the sweetest ones on the other side. Some moments of worship may feel like practice, or even like we're being hypocritical. But what if it's hypocritical to worship only when we feel like it?

Here's another way to think about it. I don't make our bed in the morning because I have to. Rather, I want the house to feel clean, together, and restful when we get home. So I push past the "I don't feel like it" lethargy and just do it. At times, it can feel similar in approaching *moments* of worship. We may have to choose to worship simply because it's the best thing, regardless of how we feel. Worship, founded in a relational place, is the overflowing response or reaction to the 'You're so good to me Papa' reality of who He is to you.

It's that simple. It always has been, and it always will be.

Rhythm of Practicing Peace

When we move from *knowing about* to *really knowing*, we see more clearly who He is. This brings us to a place of worship, or delight.

Psalm 37v4 says: "Delight yourself in the Lord and he will give you the desires of your heart."

It's a process. Delight in Him, then He'll give.

In Matthew 7v7-8 Jesus teaches His disciples to ask: "Ask and it will be given to you; seek and you will find; knock and the door will be opened to you. For everyone who asks receives; the one who seeks finds; and to the one who knocks, the door will be opened."

In John 14v13-14 Jesus again teaches His disciples to ask, but this time reveals a bit more of how it works: "Whatever you ask in My name, that will I do, so that the Father may be glorified in the Son. If you ask Me anything in my name, I will do it."

Notice the line, "*in My name.*" Or you can think about it as, "*If it lines up with who I am and what I know is best.*" So the reality is that as we delight in Him we'll know what He's like and what He wants to do.

It all comes back to delighting in the Lord. As we do, our desires get properly sorted. It's the process where His desires become ours too and the doorway for them to turn into realities because we then know what to ask.

Ask Him what it looks like for you to delight in Him today.

Write what you feel He's saying:

Worship to Receiving

If life *with God*, or life *in God*, is a process like any relationship then there must be a general next direction in which it can head. This book is written with hopes to help your journey shift from god to Abba, then in that place… to a life of worship. As we continue going deeper in our longing to really know what God is like, I believe the next step is one of receiving.

Relationally, receiving can be both tangible and intangible.

It's about things *and* thoughts.

Provision in physical lack *and* words that create, define, and set us free.

Receiving from our Father happens the moment His delight is transferred (or becomes real) to us. Remember, everything God said to humanity in the garden was true, but it had to be received in order to be experienced. Therefore, the next heart posture we'll practice is *hands out*, one where we're ready to receive. It's what was always intended for us and where what already belongs to us becomes ours.

One of the most remarkable things to me about life in God is that He's longing for us to enter into a never ending eternal tide of bliss with Him. His end goal isn't us worshiping Him in the clouds some day, a common misunderstanding of "heaven." His heart isn't for us to become mindless singing robots with mouths, like speakers, aimed at Him as He sits back in some giant chair while eating grapes, arrogantly taking it all in. That's not our Abba.

Rather, He wants a relationship with us where He gives and we receive, then we give and He receives. He's that good.

Jesus painted the picture over and over by His ridiculous explanations of grace that were beyond logic or reason, but that's what God is like.

Receiving is less about *getting* and more about an in and out, back and forth, breathing in His glory and exhaling His worship kind of thing. Receiving and a life of worship go hand in hand. He loves, loves, loves, it when His kids say, "Daddy, what's next!?" Never forget that He delights in you… not because of anything you've done, but because your very existence was set into motion by a Love whose greatest intention was for you to experience His glory.

So, what if it's true? What if Jesus really is God? What if He really did swing heaven's[32] doors wide open for anyone that would believe? And what if believing is as simple as He said in Matthew 18v3?

"I tell you the truth, unless you change and become like little children, you will never enter the kingdom of heaven."

Could it be that simple? Could it be that He's just asking us to trust Him? To believe that He's telling us the truth?

I think so.

The challenge is trying to break through the tangled mess in our minds that, like a dam, stands between us and our willingness to receive what He's saying. It's a collection of wrong thoughts, hurts, and confusion that have slowly been knit together into something which makes receiving difficult.

This dam can look different for each of us, but finds an all too regular home in humanity. For some, it's wondering if you've ever *really* heard

God's voice. For others it's a hurt, a very deep hurt, that seems impossible for reconciliation or restoration. It can be confusion, as you hear conflicting things about who people think God is. Sometimes it's the clutter of feeling like life is meaningless, so convinced being done with it is the best option (if that's you... don't give up, keep going. You will make it). And still for other's... fear, anger, or anxiety crowds the highway that's intended as a pathway with God, leaving no room to even consider an Abba-like relationship with Him.

But regardless of what it may be for you, remember this: its power to control you has been broken. Its authority to consume you is null. Jesus is bigger and you are in Him.

If any of this clicks with you right now, I'd encourage you to ask Holy Spirit to set you free from whatever it is that's consuming your thoughts. He already knows about it and still loves you. Shame and guilt are not from Him. Jesus is grace. He's that good. When we honor issues by giving an excuse, we're giving them more power over us. Humble honest clarity is key. Name it for what it is, ask for Him to heal you, then wait. The most difficult part can be waiting. But you're not alone.

It can be uncomfortable to not "do anything" in the process of waiting, but this is the genesis of receiving from our Father... handing control back to Him.

He longs to continue tearing down the walls in you so that you can live a free life in Him and with those around you, but it hinges on letting Him be the one to do so, not us. This is receiving.

Jesus came to show us what it looks like when lies, worries, pain, and confusion are sorted, healed, and made clear again. Breakthrough often, not always, but often, comes in a moment of returning to the freedom of trusting like a child. Freedom is who He is.

Nothing in your life is cemented so deeply that His love and power can not rush over your entire being, especially into all the hidden places, and set you free. All He asks is for you to look into His eyes.[33] To trust that He is God, that He knows you, that He cares for you, and that wholeness is coming.

He's patiently waiting for you to break down and let Him hold you… for you to release the shoulder-weight of bitterness, shame, guilt, pride, caring what others think of you, and whatever else comes to your mind that's consuming your freedom with Him and others. He is your freedom. End of story. You cannot earn or work to gain it. We receive everything good in a childlike place as we say *yes* to Him.

—

Rhythm of Practicing Peace

Picture yourself standing in a dry valley, your mouth parched and your body aching for water, only moments away from loosing your ability to stand.

As you look up, you see a thick glass wall from one edge of the valley to the other and just on the other side is a lake brimming with pure, clear, cool water.

You notice a ladder leading up and over into the good place, but as you make your way over to it, placing your foot in the first rung, you realize your arms are full of stuff keeping you from reaching out and moving up. It's stuff you've been convinced you needed to carry, but now contrasted with the opportunity for water, it seems less important.

The anxiety of deciding whether to continue holding it and stay in that waterless place or letting it fall down, leaving it behind, and climbing the ladder… this is your decision.

With that picture in mind, what are you holding that you need to release (may be thoughts or life patterns) in order to receive God's goodness to you?

If you long for His refreshing presence to wash over you… then tell Him. If you long to know His freedom, and rest, and calm… then tell Him. You may want to open your hands or arms as a physical way agreeing with your heart in this moment.

Prayer: Jesus, I believe Your way is best. Thank you for always inviting me into more. Show me what's in the way of receiving what You have for me right now.

—

As we grow in relationship with God to a life of inhaling grace and exhaling worship, we'll arrive at a place called receiving. When God gives to us, it's directly from who He is. Which is to say, when we receive from Him, we're accessing everything we'd otherwise had no ability to access.

My beautiful wife Hillary and I don't own a helicopter, but we do have friends who own a helicopter. So when they called a few months ago asking if we wanted to go flying, we jumped at their kind offer and quickly accepted.

What was happening?

We were being given access to something we'd otherwise have no access to, simply by *receiving*.

The God who created the world is inviting us to come close to Him and access all of who He is. The Gospel and receiving go hand in hand. Like a life of worship, receiving from our Father is an ongoing life rhythm.

To some, this may sound selfish, as if we only want God for what He has to offer. But I think it's possible for this to be either good or not good depending on our understanding of God, us, and how we think about both.

Wanting what God has to offer can be destructive if it's about our immediate happiness. This thinking establishes God as a cosmic vending machine. Religion. We do "A" then we get "B."

But it's possible that wanting "more of God"[34] because of what He gives us can actually be a good thing. There's a far deeper and more mature idea at work here and it's super important to catch. The key is remembering that what God offers is Himself. His presence *is* the ultimate everything. To long for greater awareness, sensitivity, and experience of His goodness in a special way can actually be helpful.

"If you then, though you are evil, know how to give good gifts to your children, how much more will your Father in heaven give the Holy Spirit to those who ask Him!" Luke 11v13

Notice the "gift" our Abba gives us is Holy Spirit.

The person.

The Spirt of God.

Until His presence is enough for us, I'd argue we'll never feel like He's actually as good as the Scriptures say He is.

He Himself is the very best possible response to our request. This isn't how most of us have been taught to think. We've grown up being told we can do anything if we put our mind to it and work hard. We've been indoctrinated with the idea we can fix tangible things and talk through emotional ones. Our two options are to work it out or bury it deeper... either way, we can do it ourselves.

But this is a form of dualism.

Rather than seeing all of life as life with God, we separate it into smaller pieces which unintentionally restricts God from certain parts (in our minds). This thinking has subtly eroded our willingness to approach and interact with God when it comes to certain situations in our life. It halts the receiving because in our minds, He's not a part of the equation.

So often we think we know what we want.

We're sick so we think we need physical healing. We have bills so we immediately think we need money. And on and on. We're doers. Intuitive. Smart. We can figure out the solution ourselves to all of life's issues regardless of whether they're physical or emotional. And all of a sudden, we begin assuming we know what God should give us with no second thought that He might actually have something better in mind.[35]

"For my thoughts are not your thoughts, neither are your ways my ways," declares the Lord. "As the heavens are higher than the earth, so are my ways higher than your ways and my thoughts than your thoughts." Isaiah 55v8-9

How we think about life, and God, and "what fits where" is an indication of whether we're enjoying religion or relationship. As is often the case, we need balance. We need only to return to a childlike way of life with God (not to be confused with *childish*).

If you're sick, ask Him for healing, then wait. Let God heal you in the way He wants to (Example: Maybe through medicine, or through someone praying for you). If you're behind on the bills, ask Him for provision, then wait. But be open to what He says (Example: Changing certain lifestyle habits or humbly asking others for help).

Jesus told His disciples to ask for anything. He didn't see some parts as "holy" and others as "earthy." He just saw life as one big collection. So in teaching His followers and disciples to ask, He included all of life: "You may ask me for anything in my name, and I will do it." John 14v14

Should we ask God to provide for our physical needs? How about our desires? How about our dreams and hopes? Should I date that girl? Should I buy this dress? Should I go to college? Where should I go for college?

Yes on all accounts. All of life is included, and it's all important to Him because it is to us. We're His beloved, so every part of our lives matters to Him.

Jesus taught that our entire life is in God, therefore everything is conversation worthy to Him. I bet the enemy smiles when we think God only wants to talk about the "good churchy, Sunday, and Christian" stuff. But that's just not true.

Like we briefly looked at in the end of the previous chapter, the key to know how and what to ask of God is found in Jesus' words, "in His name." Meaning *in line* with who He is.

So how do we align with Him?

Well, we recognize He's saved, adopted, and welcomes us to call Him our Abba. We let Him make us into a people marked by a life of worship and prayer[36] as our value system reorients back to its proper place of longing for a greater awareness of His presence and voice in our everyday 24/7 life of sleeping, eating, working, studying, talking, listening, playing, laughing, crying, and everything else.

Interestingly, as we step into this rhythm, we become more informed of the brokenness around us. We begin to see the pain that brokenness is causing rather than people who irritate us. We start reallocating our energy and resources to partner with God in bringing life back to humanity, or better put... we start desiring heaven's realities to be earth's realities. We begin receiving His thoughts for us and those around us.

Since birth, He's been reminding us of our truest identity, whether we've received it yet or not. He's inviting us to live from a place of fighting *for* people, not *against* them... which is easier said then done, but this is why the former leads to the latter. It flows from grasping... from receiving... that we're *in God* and *He* is what we long for. The sweetest, best, and most blissful truth there is. He's the source.

Okay, so if this is the concept, what's the daily application?

As one who is in God, because of Jesus, did you know when the Father looks at you the words He uses to broadcast to the heavens are that you're *holy* and *blameless*? He's actually convinced you're holy.

Convinced you're blameless.

"Praise be to the God and Father of our Lord Jesus Christ, who has blessed us in the heavenly realms with every spiritual blessing in Christ. For he chose us in Him before the creation of the world to be holy and blameless in his sight. In love he predestined us for adoption to sonship through Jesus Christ, in accordance with his pleasure and will – to the praise of his glorious grace, which he has freely given us in the One he loves. In Him we have redemption through his blood, the forgiveness of sins, in accordance with the riches of God's grace that he lavished on us. With all wisdom and understanding, he made known to us the mystery of his will according to his good pleasure, which he purposed in Christ, to be put into effect when the times reach their fulfillment – to bring unity to all things in heaven and on earth under Christ."
Ephesians 1v3-10

Here's a conversation I've had with God about this very thing:

Me: *"Really? Are you kidding me? I was an idiot today… I feel so dumb."*

God: *"Yes, but you're holy."*

Me: *"Yeah, but I took what wasn't mine to take."*

God: *"Yes, but you're blameless."*

Me: *"Yeah, but… (and I run through my list of mistakes only to get to the end and He's still saying the same thing.)"*

God: *"That's not who you are. You're holy and blameless."*

Me: *"Why God!? Why won't you stop!? Just give me what I deserve!"*

God: *"Nathaniel, don't be afraid. Be still. I am telling you what you received from Me. Grace and freedom and life. I'm stable. Who you are isn't based on, or does not flow from, your changing emotions. It cannot work that way. I am your stability and authority. Now, let go of your excuses, they don't work with me. The sooner you do, the sooner you'll experience freedom and the sooner you can receive what I have for you today."*

You see, relationship with Him can't help but move you into a life of *worship* and *receiving* with Him. He becomes your priority, and because of it, you'll actually find yourself living His way.

But what does it mean to know in your head, then move to receiving in your heart, that you're holy and blameless in His sight? That you're safe, hidden, and secure in Him? How do those words become tangible realities in your life? This is a question I hear often, phrased in many different ways, but always the same desire. "I want to hear His voice, and I want to know how to accept all the stuff He says about me."

For many, this a point of frustration, irritation, or discouragement. We see certain people, seemingly without effort, "hearing God's voice," and we're left feeling second rate or like we did something wrong to make God angry with us… resulting in the silent treatment. If that's where you're at right now, you're not alone. Please know those people, the one's who seem to effortlessly hear God's voice, go through the same thoughts. The effects of sin are real and have dramatically affected our ability to connect with our Creator, but God made a way, through Jesus, to again interact with Him, and now by Holy Spirit we can tune into His whisper.

He longs for you to hear His voice.

He longs to be your friend.

He actually likes you.

And you're closer than you may think.

While we're all unique, I think there are a few core ideas which tend to be helpful in moving forward in this area.

First, set time aside each day to tell Him you're ready to listen. Tell Him how you long to hear His voice. Then leave room to just listen, as if you were in a conversation with someone.

We give our time, money, and thoughts to what we value most, so choose to give your thoughts to Him. And, here's the hard part... be okay with not hearing an immediate response, this may be part of *faith* for you (for now.)

Next, ask a few people to join in asking with you, for you. And pray there, on the spot. Don't accept an "I'll be praying for you." This can be humbling, but I believe necessary. If it's difficult or embarrassing, He may be uncovering a system of thought that could be hindering your conversational life with Him. God reveals in order to heal, never to shame. God in Himself is a community (Father, Son, and Holy Spirit) and therefore, being made like Him, we also live most fully in community.

Finally, be in the Scriptures and join a community of other Jesus people.

While there's no perfect Bible reading plan out there, and surely no requirement from God to find it, you'll grow in recognizing His tone, which will make distinguishing His voice from the others less of a battle. We'll explore a few ideas relating to this in Part Two, specifically in the chapter called *Reading the Scriptures.*

And by joining a community of Jesus people, I mean structuring your life to be alongside other people who want the same thing. Many people go to church gatherings, but have yet to give their lives to those in the community. It's easy to hide in a big group, but individualism can act as a thick curtain between your perception of hearing God's voice and your confidence to know it's Him.

All that said, be encouraged. He sees your heart and knows your longings. Keep seeking, He will be found by you, it's a promise: "You will seek me and find me when you seek me with all your heart." Jeremiah 29v13

As we live wanting to know God, we'll come to the core reality that we're designed for a life of worship. We're already doing it, it's nothing new, but the constant barrage of people, life situations, tangible (and intangible) stuff that's constantly after our worship can easily distract us.

We move from thinking about God as a far off unknowable one ("a god") into a place of knowing Him as our Abba (our right here, right now, Daddy). Then we move to cultivating a life a of worship, the constant awareness of His presence which leads to the overwhelming experience of His heart for us. From there we can't help but direct our attention, mind, will, and emotions toward His goodness. A life of receiving is the extension from there.

Who do you need Him to be for you?

Tell Him. Then let Him be God and choose to believe His way and response is the best possible option.

A few months ago I was staying in Black Butte, Oregon over the weekend which happens to be one of my favorite places on the planet. The high desert landscape and those tall skinny birch trees with leaves that shimmer in the wind (it looks like someone dumped glitter all over them) are my favorite.

During one of the evenings my emotions shifted and I had an urge to turn on the TV to look for something raunchy (just being honest) and very clearly heard the enemy whispering to go for it. He knew I was alone and said, "no one will find out." I instantly remembered two days earlier when I interacted with a guy who I'm fairly convinced was afflicted and bound by the enemy.

I had pulled up to a grocery store and saw a man sitting against the front wall. As I went over to see if I could do anything for him he made grumbling sounds, noting he didn't want to be bothered. So I went inside, bought food, and came back to my car. I asked Abba if He wanted me to do anything for the man. I didn't hear Him say anything specific, so I sent a text to two friends. Almost immediately, two responses came back… both said, "love Him."

I walked up again and asked his name. This time, after fighting back and forth between voices (two very distinct personalities) he looked up at me with one eye open. He was yelling, but his mouth was closed. He then opened his mouth and referred to himself as *such and such* (sounded like a demonic name to me) telling me he was "the god of fire." I'm not sure how else to explain it, but in my minds eye, I saw what looked like a black figure standing between me and a small child (this man). It was an odd experience, but I very strongly felt like he was being held captive and I wanted to see him set free. I didn't sense that Holy Spirit was leading me to do anything specific yet so I offered to make him a sandwich (sometimes practical love is the key in waiting for Holy Spirit to speak.) He went back to yelling with his mouth closed and gave me a strong "no" look to my sandwich question. I told him Jesus was for him and loved him then walked back to my car just a few feet away. Over the next hour or so I sat in my car and prayed for him.

I wish I could end the story by telling you there was some awesome freedom moment, but it didn't happen. What I did hear as I waited on Abba, was "your authority comes from me, but it's refined by your integrity," something I was rather confused about, seeing as it didn't make the situation any better. The guy eventually got up and walked away still yelling with his lips tightly pressed together.

Back to the moment at Black Butte… as I heard the enemy's taunt to reject God's best, I remembered what Abba had said to me the day before in front of the grocery store: "Your authority comes from me, but it's refined by your integrity." It clicked. The enemy wanted me to bow down to him, taking his words as truth over my Abba's. My faith expanded rather quickly in a moment of excitement, and I commanded the enemy to leave. The entire atmosphere shifted. The urge couldn't have been farther from me. It was like shifting from night to day.

You see, allowing God to do things His way and actually believing it's best isn't always natural or easy. I would have done things differently than Him, but He's got the eternal view in full perspective. I had to release my opinion of what was best in order to see the fullness be revealed. He gave me what I'd need ahead of time, and I questioned why it wasn't "useful" *then*. But His way was best. It's always the best.

The momentary challenges we face in life, though they *demand* our attention, do not *require* it. While they often present themselves as terrible and overwhelming, they must be viewed in the light of you being a victorious child of God. We feed them any authority they have, so by not feeding them, they will not thrive. God always has a solution and is reminding us of His riches in the face of the enemy who reminds us of our lack.

The Father views our lack as an opportunity to bless us. We have the choice to view our lack through a lens of fear (focusing on the unknown), or faith (focusing on what we know about God). When we remain fixated on fear, we miss the opportunity to experience an aspect our Father's character that we may otherwise not have seen. But when we believe God to be the sufficiency for our lack, we're opening ourselves up to let Him show us more of who He is.

In the story above, had I not waited, I may not have seen Him as *the One who gives me authority and trusts me to refine that authority by my integrity.* Resting in what God had already given me, not fighting for more, was the tipping point. The enemy thought he was about to gain authority, and he might have, if I hadn't believed my Father's words. Allowing His words to frame my perception of life and reality in that moment.

This is part of receiving. Hearing, yes... but then accepting. Activating the promise.

In the moments of challenge, remember your goal isn't fighting the enemy. Rather, it's believing what your heavenly Father already told you about who He is and who you are.

God and the enemy are not equals. Satan was a created being, but God always was and always will be. It's not a boxing match of equally skilled fighters, it's a done deal. Jesus wins. The enemy goes around prowling like a lion to cause fear, destroying anything he can.[37] But our God is the victorious Lion of Judah living in victory. So confident that Jesus *sits* at the right hand of the Father. Jesus is not anxiously pacing back and forth wondering if we'll make it through life, so we don't have to either.

May you, in continuing to grow as a God worshiper, move into a lifestyle of constantly receiving what your heavenly Father says about you.

—

Rhythm of Practicing Peace

What has God been saying to you about who He is for you, and how could meditating on it change your reality?

You may want to sit still in a quiet place, asking Him to remind you. You may want to pull out past journals or notebooks, flipping through all the things you've written down. You may want to look through your Bible and take note of all the underlined verses. You may want to call your best friend and ask them what they've seen God doing in your life.

Whatever it is, create space, giving all of who you are to gathering up the scattered pieces of God's direct thoughts toward you and begin to receive them all over again.

Part Two: Move

"For in Him we live and *move* and have our being." Acts 17v28a

In God, we *live. Living*, like breathing, may be described as the unseen thoughts we hold which outline our life in God.

We come to a place of agreement with who He says He is and who He wants to be for us. This agreement changes the way we think about God. It changes the way we think about ourselves and others. And in turn, it changes the way we interact with, and allow ourselves to be interacted with, all that is God.

We can enjoy real life, a kind that's worthy of the definition. And we get to receive, over and over, the endless bliss of the kingdom of God.

So we live and breathe… the internal, unseen stuff, but we also *move*. We find ourselves in constant motion. Sitting, standing. Right arm, left. Looking this way, then that. And even still, these motions, though different from our thoughts, are also *in God*. Seen and unseen… both in God.

Part Two will aim at expanding our practices in life with God. The everyday stuff you can apply.

As you read Part Two, may you know you're blessed among humanity because you're safe, secure, and loved by God. And may new patterns and routines, beautiful and restful ones, become your new normal.

Learning to Listen

Like being in a busy intersection full of cars, buses, and people all forcing their way in different directions, we too can get lost in the chaos of conflicting thoughts and become unsure of our true identity. Our soul can become overwhelmed with an overload of unprocessed thoughts making it difficult to hear God's voice.

This is a familiar, yet sadly common, experience and reality for many of us.

In this place, I've found that listening feels more like standing under a heavy waterfall than a refreshing mist. But I wonder if we've just misplaced our ability to have honest conversations with God and each other because of the constant sound we subscribe to around us.

We can easily settle into feeling safe when surrounded by a constant clutter of information. Background music, endless noisy marketing, and the buzz of cascading notifications from the phone in our pocket. All playing a part in providing cheap thrills to feed our desire for *something* to be happening around us.

But when was the last time you felt okay sitting in silence with a friend?

When was the last time you sacrificed a good chunk of your day to just sit in God's presence, asking nothing in return? Not for a feeling or to get an answer, but to *just be*.

It's become natural for many of us to say *yes* to more than we should. Multitasking and staying busy, all the while not adding up the cost. But these costs turn into consequences before we know it, creating a new normal that I believe is disrupting our ability to more clearly hear God's voice.

This way of living has, is, and will continue to throw into disorder our relational capacity to know God (and each other) in the fullness He longs for us to enjoy. But it's never too late to again learn to listen.

I believe His voice can be heard in any context if we'll listen. And I'd suggest *everything* can point to His character and goodness if we let it.

Yesterday I was eating a cucumber and noticed the inside was a triangle with a seed in the middle. I was reminded of the divine dance, of where He says I am (in Him), and because of that, I was moved to worship. God can use whatever moment we're in to talk to us. Even when sitting on a sofa eating a cucumber. This is what I mean by all of life is in God.

What would it look like to consider the loudness of our surroundings that are pushing against our souls, compromising our stillness and peace? To identify and put back into their place the crowded sounds of life that are hindering our ability to hear His tone.

Matt Stinton sings a song that's profoundly simple in nature and paints a fantastic picture of the place from which we're able to begin listening.

"There is no striving
There is no striving in Your love
Freely You have given
Freely You have given to us

You have made us Yours

You have called us daughters and sons
This is who You are
This is what Your love has done

You have given everything my heart could ever need
And all You ask is I believe
So I am resting safe inside your promise to provide
And nothing could ever change Your love
Your love for me

You never ask that I earn Your affection
I could never earn something that's free
I never have to fight for Your attention
Because Your eyes are ever upon me"

So this is where we get to start as we again learn to hear His voice.

As we return to the elemental good news that Jesus came to show us, we're reminded that we are indeed close to Him, no longer separate. It's here we can begin to receive His thoughts over us.

Am I willing to be still and listen without expecting to get anything from God in return?

It's fascinating to listen to people young and old, talk about what God is showing and teaching them. For the most part, those who live a life of love seem to express things in simple terms. They talk about elementary realities such as God's love, His grace, and His beauty. I think there's something for us to catch in that. Even in His old age the apostle John, the one who laid his head against Jesus,[38] referred to himself as "the one Jesus loved"[39] (which has also been translated as *the beloved*). He was known to travel from church to church in his old age simply teaching about love. That's it.

From someone who walked and talked with Jesus, he took away *love* as the key.

Receiving, then giving.

Breathing in, then out.

What I find fascinating is God doesn't graduate us into "higher and more complex" understandings of space and time and love. Instead the complex things become simple.

The enemy is a complicator, but Jesus is the great clarifier. As we learn to hear God's voice, everything comes back to love, which leads us to the ongoing response of, "Jesus... I just want more of Him." We can replace goal oriented thinking about life with God with an expectation to experience Him. What if God is simply maturing us into a people of love? And what if learning to listen to His whisper is the key?

For the impatient, that may not be enough. "What about the *deep* things of God!?" they may say. To which I believe Jesus would reply, "Follow me, learn my ways, and listen to my voice. It's that simple." As simple as saying *yes*, learning to wait for Him to speak. Its simplicity can be uncomfortable because it suggests the possible loss of control within religious systems.

I absolutely love how Jason Upton says it, "Love is a dangerous word to those who fear losing control."[40]

Wow.

For those of us addicted to control, that's a wake-up phrase. A profound way of explaining a Kingdom principle. Am I actually willing to listen and obey no matter what He says, or am I only hearing what I want to hear? That's the difference that can move us to a place of handing over control.

For me, it sounds a lot like this:

"Father, here's my control of _____ , take it. I give up my ability to judge myself and _____ . I *want to want* you more than I want the illusion of control over my life. Help."

I wonder what percentage of us, as a people steeped in a Western mindset,[41] are driven by the fear of losing control? And how does this fear change the way you and I hear what our heavenly Father is patiently whispering to us?

I used to think consumerism was our nation's greatest sin. Now I think it's far more relational, constantly sleeping with the prostitute of control because she promises we can be god.

Listening is relational. It's takes two parties, and in our case, listening to the voice of God can be fantastically, wonderfully, and unapologetically more simple than we make it. He does all the heavy lifting, so we release our efforts to make something happen and just be. Letting our guards, expectations, and most of all desire for control... down. We make the choice for God to be our God.

We let Him speak when and how He wants... then we wait.

We ask, then we wait.

Waiting is the clearing of space for new words. It's a form of creation, the fashioning of a greater capacity and expanse for new ideas to be given authority to grow. *Waiting* is the necessary process in time as a seed becomes a flower. *Waiting* is a beautiful part of life with God.

But we like to rush things. Same day delivery and microwaves prove my point. Yet time cannot be the scale by which we value God's response, that is far too small of a view of God.

What about a moment of life and death? How about one of extreme emotional pain or lack? In those moments, it's easy to wonder if God even cares, or if He's even real.

Totally, I agree. It feels like hell to wait in *those* moments.

But He encourages us to be honest in conversation with Him. All emotions are fair game, they don't scare Him away or blemish the way

He thinks about us. David, one author of the Psalms, was extremely candid with God to an almost uncomfortable degree.[42]

In the terrible moments, it's okay to say, "God... I *want to want*." As in, "I know what I *should* want, but I don't. I'm numb, turned off from all things I can't control, and honestly don't care." And it's okay to feel that way. But remember our feelings and perceptions don't dictate the realities of God and us in Him. If they did, that would mean we could control God.

There will be times where we have to fight to remember the simple truth that He wants the best for us. The enemy will always question the perception we have of our Father. Think about Genesis 3. The enemy's tactic was to convince humanity that *what God said to them* wasn't the fullest truth.

So how do we get, or stay, grounded in our understanding of who God *really* is so that we can hear His voice most clearly?

I suggest through the Scriptures *and* each other. We need both. And in both, we need Holy Spirit to sort it out for us.

The Scriptures act as our map, but not our destination. The story of God helps us see the world more closely to the way He does, reminding us what is most real. We're intended to make the journey through our days in constant conversation with Holy Spirit, experiencing every moment in the framework of heaven as it collides with our mind, will, and emotions. And as we spend time reading and discussing the Scriptures we'll become more expectant for what's ahead and for His victory right around the corner in every situation of life.

Proverbs 21v17-19a says:

"Pay attention and listen to the sayings of the wise; apply your heart to what I teach, for it is pleasing when you keep them in your heart and have all of them ready on your lips. So that your trust may be in the LORD."

Did you notice the "so that" statement?

"*So that* your trust may be in the LORD."

Why read the Scriptures?

Why study them?

Why apply them?

Because as we do, a shift takes place. A shift from trusting ourselves to trusting Him. The Scriptures act as a relational connection for us to know God through story.

So there's that. But we need each other as well. Because even if the physical hand of God wrote the Bible, we'd still disagree on what certain things meant. So we need each other to work through what God's heart is for us through the text and agree that some things may not be worth dividing over. That love covers the gaps of uncertainty.

May we continue to practice the art of listening. And may we let God expand the vocabulary He uses with us by recognizing all moments are "God moments."

—

Rhythm of Practicing Peace

To truly listen, we must long to know what the other has to say. To lay our systems of thought down, acknowledging we don't know everything. This is also true in our relationship with God.

Find a 12-24 hour timeframe where you can be silent, refraining from speaking.

Like fasting, the practice of silence can be cleansing. A reset. It may mean you take a vacation day, and most certainly will mean turning your phone off... don't worry, you'll live. You may find it easier to start by minimizing the amount of content you consume. If possible, avoid news, texts, social media, etc. In this practice, silence includes refraining from airing your opinions online.

Begin your time in conversation with God by simply saying, "Father, here I am. Your son/daughter is listening."

As you finish, jot down what you feel He taught you in the silence:

Learning to Talk

A while back, I learned something I hope never to forget as I listened to two friends pray.[43] I was invited into yet another facet of interaction with God.

As they prayed over me, they asked Abba questions anytime we got stuck, and to be honest, at times it felt a bit odd. I remember seeing an owl and having no idea if it was the Spirit speaking, or some random thought. But as we pressed in deeper, leaving pride behind, the Spirit spoke powerfully shaping words over my life that day. That was the day I learned what it looked like to talk with the Father in freedom.

While I wasn't aware of it prior to that moment, I began to see a road block between the Father and I. I'd entered a rhythm of looking for answers from God more than I was after just enjoying our relationship.

When we speak with God, I think it's easy to do so with an expectation of what will happen. And while this may be natural, it has the potential to direct the conversation and assumed outcome… thus making us the 'god' in the conversation.

Here's an example:

You have a decision to make, so you ask, "God… what should I do about _____?"

Or, you need to know which option to choose in a specific situation, so you pray something like, "God, I need direction on which _____ to choose."

So He says something by bringing a verse to mind, a person, a thought, a memory, a picture, or one of the other endless ways He chooses to communicate with us.

But if you don't know what it means, or if you don't get a black and white response… what do you do? What if a yellow school bus comes to mind?

What if instead of, "Choose _____," you hear, "wood table?" What do you do with that?

In those moments, it's easy to assume He didn't say anything because we only gave Him room to say *this* or *that.* It's simple enough to come to the conclusion that He's being silent and a random thought has surfaced in your mind.

But what if that "wood table" is the start of an adventure of conversation with Him? What if He's actually beginning a conversation with you? What if the *give and take, breathing in and out,* realities of life with God apply to your conversations with Him too?

I don't know of a single healthy, growing, beneficial relationship on the planet that operates with one word or phrase responses. That kind of relationship sounds cold, distant, and selfish to me. Very different than the heart of God toward us.

I remember a story from a few years ago about this very thing.

As a group of us were praying with a friend, I silently asked Abba if there was anything He wanted to say through me to this person. Rather quickly the words, "father to the fatherless" came to mind. So instead of stopping there, I quietly asked Abba what it meant.

The conversation was simple. It sounded something like this, "Abba, what does *father to the fatherless* mean or have to do with our friend?"

Then I saw, in my mind's eye, our friend wearing what looked like an Ironman suit. If at this point you think I'm going crazy, no problem. But have you read the Scriptures? The interactions people have with God are pretty odd at times.

So again I asked, "Abba, why the suit of armor?"

I felt like He said our friend was being given some sort of ability. I wasn't sure how to share this, so as others prayed and listened I kept asking Abba questions.

Simple ones. The kind of questions children ask, because Jesus said, "Truly I tell you, unless you change and become like little children, you will never enter the kingdom of heaven." Matthew 18v3

Eventually it came around full circle. I felt like God was saying our friend was about to be given an ability from the Father to be a father to the fatherless, and that their experience of a father's love through our friend would acts as a door for them to meet their heavenly Father for the first time.

So I shared it, willing to be totally off, but do you know what happened?

A few minutes after the group was done praying, our friend came over to me. Apparently another guy in the group shared a similar thing with him right after. The thoughts lined up, and our friend was encouraged. He was reminded in that moment that God sees him and knows him and has a hope and a future for him.

I think that's one way life with Abba can look.

This is what my two friends (at the start of this chapter) helped me see was missing. Rather than asking for answers or for Him to validate one of our three options for Him to choose from, what if we became a people who were willing to engage in childlike conversation with Him? A conversation that more resembles a Thanksgiving dinner than a microwave meal?

He knows you and will speak in ways you can understand. For some, pictures. For others, feelings. And on and on. But never forget the point is *always* relationship with Him. It's *always* about the exchange. Even as He speaks, it's not about the "word," but about His heart being known through the word.

This way of interacting with God can be more confusing than helpful for some. It might make them uncomfortable or skeptical, and I get that. My suggestion is to be in the Scriptures often and avoid trying to always "get God to say something." Instead, telling God you're open to Him talking with you in whatever way He wants is a good heart posture to maintain.

May we learn to move from talking *at* God to talking *with* Him. And may we be willing to ask Him questions about what He says in hopes to know His heart for us and others, more fully.

—

Rhythm of Practicing Peace

Prayer: God, I'm not fully sure about all this, but I do know I want more of You. So right here and right now I declare that I'm open to You speaking to me in any way You want. Here I am, Your son/daughter is listening.

Throughout today, remind yourself He's with you as you ask Him to show you more of who He is.

Learning to Trust

If everything our Father says to us is true, then believing the truth is a relational response. And similarly, if everything the enemy says to us is a distortion of the truth, then believing lies is an alternative relational response. Whether we believe the truth or lies is a matter of whom we're choosing to trust.

Lies act as a corrosive agent to our mind, will, and emotions because their core motive is bringing us to ruin. The damage they can cause is insane, so of course the enemy has spent his time learning the craft of delivering really great sounding ones.

Let's work through a 30,000 foot overview of what lies are and how they play into our life in God.

Just the other day, while driving on the freeway, I began to smell burning rubber. My first thought was that it was my car. "Did something just go wrong?" I asked myself. For a moment, I considered pulling over. I was hearing, "Your car is broken, it's going to cost a lot of money, you're toast man." But as I took an inventory of what was going on around me, I noticed a semitruck not too far ahead that was downshifting, quickly coming to a stop. That's when I realized the burning rubber smell was from the truck, not from my car. And so my mind again returned to a calm and stable place.

It's been said our minds can be the enemy's playground, and I would agree. A correct thought can lead to faithfulness, integrity, and consistency. But a wrong thought can do a fine job of convincing us that making an irrational decision is actually a good idea when it's definitely not.

C.S Lewis, in his book *The Screwtape Letters*, unpacks lies in an incredibly helpful way. He walks through some of the common lies we hear and helps us view them in a greater, more eternal perspective.

Unfortunately, what's true and untrue usually commingles in our thinking which makes separating them difficult. But as Jesus people, it's super important we stay aware of the thoughts we're subscribing to in order to identify the lies, expose the layers, uncover the root, and allow God to rescue us from them by telling us the truth.

God is radical about dealing with the sin in our lives because in our sin, we're delighting in lies. He longs for us to know more of who He is. And as we recognize His kindness, we'll be led to repentance (changing our thinking about what is good).

We've already won the fight, but at the same time we're right in the middle of it. The paradoxes of life in God, here and now, are unfathomable, but beautiful. It's these unexplainable balances that result in fresh thinking about how amazing God really is, giving new definitions and expressions of hope. And as Holy Spirit is our guide and teacher, we'll experience the brilliant hope of working through everything we encounter in a conversation with Him and others.

"But when He, the Spirit of truth, comes, He will guide you into all the truth. He will not speak on his own; He will speak only what He hears, and He will tell you what is yet to come." John 16v13

I find it fascinating that we see little to nothing in the darkness, but when a light is switched on everything changes. I wonder if today, God is wanting to give you this picture as one to remind you of who He is for you. A picture of feeling trapped in a dark place that suddenly becomes illuminated, revealing that the oppression you felt was flowing from what you thought was true in the dark based on a false perception of what you imagined was there, but that you're actually in an open and spacious place.

Lies produce fear, but light exposes truth. And the Light has come into the world to show us again what is true. Jesus is the light. His very presence pushes out darkness. This is another aspect of who He wants to be for you.

"When Jesus spoke again to the people, he said, "I am the light of the world. Whoever follows me will never walk in darkness, but will have the light of life." John 8v12

–

Rhythm of Practicing Peace

Prayer: Jesus, at certain moments I feel the darkness of confusion. I feel trapped and oppressed in _____ (specific area of your life). I'm confused, lonely, and hurting.

But here and now, I give my entire life back to You again, show me the truth again God. I want to walk in the light like You said I could. I want to be free. I change my thinking about what's best and say Your way is better even when I don't understand. Here's my trust. I want to walk with You in the light today.

Thank you for always wanting to set me free. I say *yes* to You today.

–

The enemy takes something that's true, swaps out a word or two, or moves punctuation around, and the confusion begins.

Take this for example:

The phrase, "Go to the store," vs "Got to the store."[44]

The smallest detail… in this case adding a "t," changes the entire meaning. And that's one of the enemy's first and most successful tactics with us: *confusion*.

Confusion moves us to ask questions concerning the elementary truths about God and ourselves so they become blurry. Does God *really* love me? Have I *gone too far* for Him to still care about me? How could God use me *after all this*?

God has given us everything we need to live a full free life,[45] starting and ending in our relationship with the Father. It's here that our greatest tool for separating lies from truth exists. His voice is like the light that shows us what's really going on. But asking the Father to speak is only half the equation. Our posture of preparing to receive or reject what He says is the other half.

Lies can become like our friends, when we get emotionally attached to them, it can feel like a personal attack if they're questioned. This is because lies, much like truth, grow deeper in us over time. So, like an extensive root system being ripped out from the ground, it can be painful to work through them. But this is why trusting God to be *good, perfect, and deeply in love with you* is so important. It will be your greatest help in sustaining your willingness to continue forward in the process towards healing.

Have you ever asked a friend's opinion on something, but already had something in mind you wanted to hear? Regardless of what they said, your mind was already made up?

I think we do this with our heavenly Father sometimes. At least I do.

There's an incredible word picture in the Hebrew Scriptures regarding "integrity" that I think explains this concept well.

In Exodus, we read about the high priest wearing a special set of clothes as he approached God's presence.

Now this may sound odd, but remember, everything finds its place within a context. Here, the special clothing acted as an identifier to the people that the LORD was holy, or set apart.

One piece of the clothing was a plate that hangs over his chest, literally referred to as a "breastplate." We see a similar item mentioned in the New Testament by Paul in Ephesians 6, referring to standing firm in the truth of God as the enemy comes against us. This breastplate had something called a *Thummim* on it.

"Also put the Urim and the Thummim in the breastpiece, so they may be over Aaron's heart whenever he enters the presence of the Lord. Thus Aaron will always bear the means of making decisions for the Israelites over his heart before the Lord." Exodus 28v30

Stick with with me here. This is incredible...

The Hebrew word for integrity is "tummah" which comes from the word "thummim." Or in other words, the high priest would approach God with "integrity" over his "heart." Symbolic, yes, but powerful. You see, when the high priest asked God what to do, whatever God said became *the* way. There was no second option.

Which raises a question. When we ask God something, are we asking just to get His opinion, or are we asking in hopes to hear the undeniable best answer with every intention to look past our feelings and believe He is who He says He is, that He's trustworthy? That's integrity. And it's when we ask *with integrity* that He'll direct us.

He knows the games we play, all our tricks, yet still desires for us to let Him take us further into knowing His love. He really is compassionate and gracious, slow to anger, abounding in love and faithfulness, maintaining love to thousands, and forgiving wickedness, rebellion and sin (Exodus 34v6-7a).

Rhythm of Practicing Peace

Take a few minutes to read Psalm 139 (below) and ask Him to search your heart. Here's what the conversation could start like:

"Father thank you for always knowing what's best for me. I want to trust what You say. So right now, I confess that sometimes I come to You unprepared to obey, but today I'm choosing to change that. Show me how to be a person of integrity with You. I love You. Thank you for loving me first."

"You have searched me, Lord,
and you know me.
You know when I sit and when I rise;
you perceive my thoughts from afar.
You discern my going out and my lying down;
you are familiar with all my ways.
Before a word is on my tongue
you, Lord, know it completely.
You hem me in behind and before,
and you lay your hand upon me.
Such knowledge is too wonderful for me,
too lofty for me to attain.

Where can I go from your Spirit?
Where can I flee from your presence?
If I go up to the heavens, you are there;
if I make my bed in the depths, you are there.
If I rise on the wings of the dawn,
if I settle on the far side of the sea,
even there your hand will guide me,
your right hand will hold me fast.
If I say, "Surely the darkness will hide me
and the light become night around me,"
even the darkness will not be dark to you;
the night will shine like the day,
for darkness is as light to you.

For you created my inmost being;
you knit me together in my mother's womb.
I praise you because I am fearfully and wonderfully made;
your works are wonderful,
I know that full well.
My frame was not hidden from you
when I was made in the secret place,
when I was woven together in the depths of the earth.
Your eyes saw my unformed body;
all the days ordained for me were written in your book
before one of them came to be.
How precious to me are your thoughts, God!
How vast is the sum of them!
Were I to count them,
they would outnumber the grains of sand;
when I awake, I am still with you.

If only you, God, would slay the wicked!
Away from me, you who are bloodthirsty!
They speak of you with evil intent;
your adversaries misuse your name.
Do I not hate those who hate you, Lord,
and abhor those who are in rebellion against you?
I have nothing but hatred for them;
I count them my enemies.
Search me, God, and know my heart;
test me and know my anxious thoughts.
See if there is any offensive way in me,
and lead me in the way everlasting."

—

You're intended to live in a place of blessing. Blessing that is defined by receiving everything in the open hand of your Father.

Proverbs 10v24 says, "What the wicked dread will overtake them; what the righteous desire will be granted."

Or, those who choose to reject God ("the wicked" means *against God or man*) will live in a place of fear, or dread. But those who repent (change their thinking, turning again towards God's face) and receive all God is for them can live in a place of anticipating constant blessing.

Fear doesn't exist in Him.

"There is no fear in love. But perfect love drives out fear, because fear has to do with punishment. The one who fears is not made perfect in love." 1 John 4v18

And you're *in* Him.

"On that day you will realize that I am in my Father, and you are in me, and I am in you." John 14v20

That's the point, to remember you're in that place, in Him. This is the strategy of heaven to break lies. Here, rather than lies being stuffed deeper only to cause pain later, they're addressed by God and replaced by the truth. All we have to do is agree.

Again, lies produce fear. The fear of someone finding out, of not being accepted, of failing, of not being good enough, etc. The lie that you're the only one who has failed, who feels this way, or that you've made a mistake too big to fix. But that's not who you are. That's living in fear, not love. Fear produces an identity mix up as we choose to embrace it. Fear makes us slaves, but in God we're free because we're accepted and deeply loved.

"So you are no longer a slave, but God's child; and since you are his child, God has made you also an heir." Galatians 4v7

You're destined to be set free. Are you ready? Jesus has come to set *all* prisoners free and today is your day. Your camp is being liberated as He welcomes you into freedom. All you need to do is let Him show you the way.

His story, the same story we find ourselves in, reminds us over and over that He's given everything to redeem us from darkness and brought us into the light. "For he has rescued us from the dominion of darkness and brought us into the kingdom of the Son he loves." Colossians 1v13

This means you get to live anticipating His freedom, rescue, provision, and presence when you desperately need it.
Love *always* keeps His promises.

Words like *grace* and *mercy* are intended to help express realities that can be difficult to accept because of their *too good to be true* nature. But this is who our Father, Jesus, and Holy Spirit is: *the wonder and love of all things.*

Lies seek to muddy the promises of God to us, but the Scriptures remind us of the place we're *really* in. That we can always seek Him.

One of my favorite reminders is in 2 Thessalonians 3v4, "May the Lord direct your hearts into God's love and Christ's perseverance." Eugene Peterson says it like this: "May the Master take you by the hand and lead you along the path of God's love and Christ's endurance."

So may the Master, our Father, lead you into God's love today. May you be reminded that nothing can separate you from His love as we begin to believe that our life is more about *receiving* and *being led* than about fighting "to get close to God." That reality won't change. He's never going to pull away from us, even when our assumptions, emotions, and forgetful minds do.

We're *good at forgetting*... but He's *better at reminding*.

The enemy schemes to convince us that our sin is too deep to deal with and managing, hiding, or burying it are the only options. But if we accept the shame and guilt we'll retreat, become stonewalled toward God and each other. We know how to create environments where we don't have to remember. We begin to believe that an imbalanced amount of something (alcohol, food, relationships, social media, movies, or whatever) will somehow make us more balanced.

Do you see the lie? The enemy delights in the momentary destruction of our willingness to remember who God is while we attempt to meet our greatest longings and needs in an illogical way. *Anything but Him.*

Our sin cannot be managed, hidden, or buried. Jesus is the great clarifier and light of life. He resets us again and again… as much as we're willing. And as we say *yes* to Him, a bud of resurrection life can begin to peak up from the soil of our soul. The lies we formerly believed must die because we're cutting off their life support and, in turn, the ground is softened, making way for new life.

Flowers cannot grow in concrete, but in tilled soft soil… they flourish.

Eugene Peterson, in his book *The Pastor*, says, "…as Karl Barth, quoting Niche pithily reminds us. Only where graves are is there resurrection. We practice our death by giving up our will to live on our own terms. Only in that relinquishment or renunciation are we able to practice resurrection."

It's in the moments of giving up our will to live on our own terms that words like *grace* and *mercy* transition from words on paper to experiences with Abba. It pushes against human logic why He'd give His life for us so that we could be with Him. But He did, and we find ourselves in the part of the story where He's giving us time to receive all that He is. And one effect of receiving Him as our King is that lies and truths get sorted. They get laid out on the table for us to address, one by one, asking Holy Spirit for help.

So the next time you find yourself choosing what you know is against God's best. Rejecting His words to you. Turning your face from His. Giving yourself to the indulgence of sin. And as moment of stolen glory wears off and you're again sober to what you just did, sick about it. Wishing you could forget. Wishing you could go back. Remember what He said in Ephesians about you:

"For he chose us in Him before the creation of the world to be holy and blameless in his sight." Ephesians 1v4

As Abba's child, He chose you. And not only that, but He see's you as *holy* and *blameless*. He has not retreated from you.

"For I am convinced that neither death nor life, neither angels nor demons, neither the present nor the future, nor any powers, neither height nor depth, nor anything else in all creation, will be able to separate us from the love of God that is in Christ Jesus our Lord." Romans 8v38-39

He came in the person of Jesus to make a way for you to be close to Him, *even while you were in sin.*

His grace toward you does not depend on you.

"You see, at just the right time, when we were still powerless, Christ died for the ungodly. Very rarely will anyone die for a righteous person, though for a good person someone might possibly dare to die. But God demonstrates his own love for us in this: While we were still sinners, Christ died for us." Romans 5v6-8

His mercy toward you does not depend on you. He delights in showing mercy.

"Who is a God like you, who pardons sin and forgives the transgression of the remnant of his inheritance? You do not stay angry forever but delight to show mercy." Micah 7v18

—

Rhythm of Practicing Peace

Prayer: Papa,

Thank you.

I knew what I was doing. I believed the lie. And I acted on it.

I turned my attention from You. I took the bait. Fell into the trap, and now I'm broken.

But You're my God. You're my redeemer.

I turn my face back toward Yours.

Ashamed and broken, but longing for You to hold me again.

You're beautiful. You're my love. All I want is You.

I worship You for never leaving. For Your grace toward me. For Your mercy toward me.

Thank You for calling me *holy*. For calling me *blameless*.

I don't want to look away from Your eyes ever again.

I only want You. Just You.

Thank You for giving me a fresh start, a new beginning. That even in my sin, You longed for me to return and see how wonderful You are.

Here I am Abba. Yours alone.

No more lies, everything I am is Yours.

—

In summary, lies are a twisting of the truth, and God longs for us to stay aware that we're safe in Him. He illuminates the lies we're believing so that we can break agreement with them and receive what He thinks about that place in our life. One of the most common lies is that we're too dirty for Him, but like we see in Ephesians, it's just not true. He *always* welcomes us to come close.

A simple way to work through the lies we've chosen to believe is to ask Him (maybe in a quiet space) what lies you're believing. Write

them out. Then break agreement with the lie by telling God you're no longer going to let that lie define you. Ask Him what He thinks about it, accept His answer, and make a new agreement.

Here's a conversional example from my talk with God this morning:

Me: "Father, what's a lie that I'm believing?"
God: "Your value comes from being better than someone else at something so that you can feel better about yourself."

Me: "Yeah, I feel that. I know it's not good."

God: "Do you want to live in freedom?"

Me: "Yes, I do."

God: "You know what to do, follow me."

Me: "Yeah, okay. God, I break agreement with believing that I'm only as valuable as I am good at things. I recognize that's not your way and I reject it being the way I choose to live. What does it look like for me to live in freedom then?"

God: "As my boy, I love you. Is that enough for you?

Me: "I need your help to believe it because the old way seems easier to prove. But I'm choosing to agree with You. That You being proud of me is enough. I accept that my value and worth comes from how You see me. I agree with You that my validation of being successful comes from resting in You. Yes. I actually feel more free now."

God: "This is how it works, I am your freedom and I love you."

May we become more and more a people who long to hear and accept what our Father thinks, rather than entertaining every idea that comes our way.

Reading the Scriptures

When it comes to reading the Bible, it's easy for a ton of great questions to surface which can hinder the pure enjoyment and beauty of taking it all in. This enjoyment and beauty is an experience and discipline we're all invited into, so it may be helpful to work through a few of our questions in hopes for them to find their proper place in our thinking.

To start… I'm a big fan of questions, especially open-ended ones that lead us deep into conversation, away from pithy, solve-all statements. **Questions can be a wonderful part of life in God if we let them. They can create space for us to embrace the wonder and pure bliss of God.**

Here are a few examples from the Scriptures:

Moses was curious at the burning bush in Exodus 3v3-4. And God used it to spark a revolution.

Ananias asked God to make sense of what He was speaking to him in Acts 9. And God used it to prophetically ignite Paul's life of love.

Even Jesus asked questions to frame a canvas to paint life onto in Mark 9v21. And God used it as a space to manifest His glory in the form of healing.

Questions can be the first step toward faith. They can be our way of admitting that we don't have all the answers. Our way of realizing and acknowledging who we really are as we come to grips with our limited understanding, knowledge, and size within the visible universe.

I'd encourage you to spend an afternoon at your local zoo and watch the faces of little kids seeing animals in real life. Just watch their eyes! Their expressions! Because whether they want to or not, they're overcome by the wonder of everything around them. I think that's where the most possibility of enjoyment in life exists. Letting our guards down, rejecting pride and caring more about experiencing God than what others might think of us. And as we spend time in the Scriptures with a desire to *know* God, we'll further return to a place of childlike wonder.

May we, like children, choose to live in wonder towards life and God. May we move from cold facts to warm fascination as questions are raised, trusting that God is bigger. That all questions find their value and place in Him. Even *questions* are in God. And in Him, there is no fear... only love.

I start there because it reminds us we're all in this together. My friend Evan says, "Our questions are often the same ones, just recycled." And when it comes to reading the Scriptures, here's a few common questions:

The Bible is a big book. Where do I start?

It seems confusing, like a ton of little stories all grouped together. What's the point of it?

The words seem old fashioned. Why does it say stuff like *thee* and *thou?*

How does an ancient story have anything to do with my life today?

All wonderful questions. This chapter is intended to hand you a few tools you can use in your everyday moments of reading that will help jump some common gaps of confusion from questions like the ones above.

So, let's start big picture, then drill down to more specifics.

First, the Scriptures are one big story divided into two parts… the Old Testament (also referred to as the Hebrew Scriptures)[46] and the New Testament.

The first part of the Bible is referred to as the Old Testament, made up of 39 smaller parts… or books. The second half is called the New Testament, made up of another 27 books. So in total, the most accepted (by scholars) Bible we have today has 66 books, starting in Genesis and ending in Revelation.

Each book is unique, but from the handfuls of authors one thing ties them all together. In some mystical way, God gave each author the inspiration to write what they did. He also gave them the freedom to do so in their own way, in a way that made sense to them.[47] This is why David, a commonly known author of many, but not all, the Psalms uses language vastly different than those of Moses in Leviticus.

There are a ton of great books that explain how we got the Scriptures. Why certain writings were included and others weren't. For time sake, we won't work though all that here. But if you're interested, be sure to check out Paul Wegner's, *The Journey from Texts to Translations* and Clinton E. Arnold's, *How We Got the Bible.*

My goal in this chapter is to help make the Scriptures more understandable and enjoyable as you read them, so let's get to work.

While in Bible college, one of my absolute favorite teachers was Ray Lubeck. He's incredibly smart, but more than that, he's one of those people you can tell have their life and teaching lined up. And because he lived what he taught, Ray was one of the most loved teachers on campus. A ton of what we'll go through in these next few pages is pulled from the structure of his book *Read the Bible for a Change.* Ray does a great job of making complex things simple and approachable. So let's start with two terms… *general* and *special revelation.*

General revelation is summarized in Romans 1v20:

"For since the creation of the world God's invisible qualities, his eternal power and divine nature, have been clearly seen, being understood from what has been made, so that people are without excuse."

It's a way of saying God speaks to us in all, and through all, especially by the visible created world around us.

Special revelation is a bit more *human*. Hebrews 1v1-2 explains:

"Going through a long line of prophets, God has been addressing our ancestors in different ways for centuries. Recently he spoke to us directly through his Son. By his Son, God created the world in the beginning, and it will all belong to the Son at the end. This Son perfectly mirrors God, and is stamped with God's nature. He holds everything together by what he says–powerful words!" (The Message)

So special revelation refers to the more (human) relationally connected ways in which God is speaking to us. One being Jesus and the other being the Scriptures, or recordings of what God has given *to* humanity *through* humanity, by His Spirit.

This is why the Scriptures are so important in the maturing of our life with God and each other. They act as a holy conversation between us and God. They're the place we see His thoughts about us in writing. The universal get-to-know God truths which shape our ability to pick Holy Spirit's voice out from among the others.

In Matthew 22v37-40 Jesus teaches us the purpose of the book. Today, this may have been equivalent to His Twitter reply to someone asking what the Scriptures are for. He says:

"Love the Lord your God with all your passion and prayer and intelligence.' This is the most important, the first on any list. But there is a second to set alongside it: 'Love others as well as you love yourself.' These two commands are pegs; everything in God's Law and the Prophets hangs from them." (The Message)

So the purpose of the Bible is to learn to live a life steeped in loving God and loving people. The Scriptures reshape our perspective of God, leading us to long for the ecstasy of His presence.

His presence, then, adjusts the way we think and live in relation to Him and those around us.

So the Scriptures are our constant reminder to the actuality of His love for us and to our ability and invitation to again and again say *yes* to Him.

Life, as seen in the Scriptures, is one. All of life is in God, both the seen and unseen.

Our emotions… and our body.

Our thoughts… and our actions.

Our hopes, dreams, planning… and our work.

Our desires… and our relationships.

It all fits into the big story, or meta-narrative, of life *in God*. This is, in my opinion, why God in Deuteronomy 31v6 (through Moses) said to Israel, "Be strong and courageous. Do not be afraid or terrified because of them, for the Lord your God goes with you; he will never leave you nor forsake you." Of course… because God doesn't give us an ongoing pass or fail. When Jesus defeated death through resurrection, He took yesterday's sin *and* tomorrow's sin. So what else is there to separate you from His love? From His presence?

Nothing.

May we continue waking up to His love.

So we read the Scriptures because they align our minds and hearts with His, but the Scriptures also remind us of what's most true in the midst of confusion.

In Luke 24, we see Jesus walking with two people (post-resurrection) listening to their deep discouragement and disappointment about how they thought He was still dead. For whatever reason, they didn't recognize it was Him.

"Then he (Jesus) said to them, "So thick-headed! So slow-hearted! Why can't you simply believe all that the prophets said? Don't you see that these things had to happen, that the Messiah had to suffer and only then enter into his glory?" Then he started at the beginning, with the Books of Moses, and went on through all the Prophets, pointing out everything in the Scriptures that referred to him." (The Message)

Life can feel great one day, then terrible the next. God knows this and because of it gave us the Scriptures as a reminder to keep putting our hope in Jesus regardless of our feelings or assumptions.

As you may have guessed, the main character in the Bible is Jesus; this includes the Father and Holy Spirit. It's all about who He is and how His life wins over our death. Each story, song, and letter in the Scriptures is Him communicating His love for us as we get a window into humanity's many responses. The pinnacle of God's love being Him coming close to us in the person of Jesus, the Messiah.

Being on the other side of Jesus' ascension back to the Father, we get to engage directly with Holy Spirit, our teacher (and much more). "But the Advocate, the Holy Spirit, whom the Father will send in my name, will teach you all things and will remind you of everything I have said to you." John 14v26

So as you read, ask *Him* to teach you: "Open my eyes that I may see wonderful things in your law." Psalm119v18

He won't hold anything good from you except that which you won't receive. I wonder if there are piles of good things He's trying to give us that we haven't said yes to yet?

He's perfect and says things like (in my own words): Here I am, come taste and see that I'm better than you could even hope. Better than any other relationship, than the feeling that comes with having money in your bank account, or having power over someone else. If you really knew how beautiful I was, you'd lay it all down. Come home. The table is set, ready for us to enjoy time together again. Nothing I have is off limits for you as you come with an open heart, mind, and life to receive it.

–

Rhythm of Practicing Peace

Spend a few minutes asking Him what He wants to give you today. And remember any perception of Him wanting to take something *from us* is actually *Him making* space for something better. There is no fear in Love. We can trust that whatever He says is always best.

Go ahead and jot down what you hear Him saying to you and what it looks like to receive it:

–

It's easier to read certain parts of the Bible than others because it's made up of three rotating types of literature. Narrative (or story), poetry (including songs), and discourse (letters, debates, talks, etc.) Each is helpful as it plays into the complete collection that is the Bible.

About 44% of the Bible is story.
33% is poems and songs.
And 22% is teachings, letters, debates, and talks.

This brings us to the topic of *context*.

Context is defined as the circumstances that create the setting for an event, statement, or idea. Context offers terms by which concepts and moments can be fully understood, assessed, and placed.

Context tells you there's a difference between when ads say, "You need this!" and when a doctor tells you the same thing. When it comes to the Scriptures (or any communication for that matter) context is not only helpful, but necessary to grasping what's really being said.

This is what most study bibles and commentaries are for. At the start of each chapter you're given certain pieces of information, such as when it was written, whom it was written for, and insight into the economic and political situation of the time. If you're interested in picking one up, I've included a few in the endnotes.[48]

Here's an example of something you'd find in a commentary, showing why context is so helpful.

When we read "Jesus Christ," it means something very different than His first and last name. Sure, today when we see two names together we think first and last, but to these people *Christ* was a title that carried a massive amount of authority. Derived from the Greek word *Christos,* it meant *Anointed One* and was linked to the word *Messiah* in Hebrew. The Messiah was the one who the Jews were waiting for to release them from oppressive Rome. They lived for the day when this powerful leader, anointed by God, would come lead the fight to physical, geographic, and religious freedom. So when people in the Scriptures referred to Jesus as the *Messiah*, or as Jesus *Christ,* they were making the connection that He was the *Anointed One of God* who had come to save them (in all areas of life). It was a big deal in their minds which is why a lot of the arguments we read about were so intense.

A few details of context like these can unlock so much for you as you read. But as a word of encouragement, don't let not having a good commentary or study Bible stop you from reading. Remember, Holy Spirit is your teacher and He'll show you everything that is good and helpful for your today. Always leading you back to Jesus.

Ray offers a few really good questions to ask as you read. Four questions we can ask to better understand the Bible.

First, what does it say?

Make practical observations.

Let's practice with John 4v7: "When a Samaritan woman came to draw water, Jesus said to her, "Will you give me a drink?"

Well, there's a woman.
She's a Samaritan.
So different groups of people exist.
She needed water.
She had a need.
She traveled to get water.
She could travel.
Jesus was there.
Jesus would have traveled to get there.
Jesus spoke to the woman.
Jesus can speak.
Jesus asks her a question.
Jesus asks questions.
Jesus is thirsty.
Jesus got thirsty.
Jesus needed water.
Jesus asked for help.

And so on. It's simple, yes, but there's power in slowing down to recognize the simple things.

Second, what does it mean?

This is where we piece together the observations we've made.
What's happening? What exchange is being made, or what does it
show us about the people involved? This is where we move from *details*
to *meaning*.

In our John 4 text, among other things, we see Jesus reaching out to
have a conversation with a woman who was different than Him. She was
a Samaritan, He wasn't. From this, we know Jesus cared more about
her knowing He was willing to be associated with her than caring what
others may have thought. He valued this woman even though others
didn't.

Third, what truths is it teaching or communicating?

The Scriptures express heaven's realities available to us in Jesus by
Holy Spirit. So what truth is being expressed by what you just read?

Note: Especially in narrative writings, context is what comes *before* and
after. So generally, try to read stories in their entirety. You can find
people saying some pretty weird stuff because they pull out lines from
the Scriptures without taking into account the context in which it's found.

If we read the John 4 story in context, we see the truth that God actually
wants to meet us in the moments when we feel alone or like we should
hide because of sin. We also see that He knows *all* our sin, yet calls us
to change our thinking (repent) and come to Him as our Savior allowing
Him to fulfill our desires.

Finally, so what? Or, how do I respond?

In this one short verse, we're welcomed into having a conversation with
God regardless of our standing with family, friends, and the people
around us. Knowing that, how does it change this moment? How do I
respond?

For me, it's thanks. "God thank you that You haven't given up on me. Thank you that You meet with me even when I feel overwhelmed or alone. Here I am Abba. I want to listen and say *yes* to what You have to say to me today."

So next time you open the Scriptures, give these four questions a try as you ask Holy Spirit to be your teacher:

What does it say?

What does it mean?

What truth is it communicating?

And how do I respond?

If you want to explore any of these four questions in more detail, be sure to check out Ray Lubeck's, *Read the Bible for a Change.*

As we read, it's helpful to ask ourselves whose voice we're wanting to hear? Closely linked with context is our *intention* in reading. The two big fancy theological words here are *exegesis* and *eisegesis.*

"Exegesis" simply means *to lead out of.* Think *Exodus,* the story of Israel *being led out of* Egypt. When each part of the Bible was written, the author had a message in mind. And while there is a degree of relativity about words, what's written was intended to communicate something. The paradox is God can use one story to say a hundred things to hundred people. But the common denominator is God. This is why we ask Him to be our teacher. The text has meaning and it's exposed by Holy Spirit as we listen.

To read the Scriptures this way is to ask Holy Spirit what He wants to say through them.

On the other hand, "eisegesis" means quite the opposite, *to lead into.*

To read the Scriptures this way is to attempt to make them agree with your opinion regardless of what it actually means. It's easy to have an opinion, then flip through the pages looking for a verse to back up what *we* think is right. Of course the danger in reading the Scriptures this way is they can become a weapon to oppress each other rather than a key to set each other free. As we read, may our intention be to gather from the text what God is saying, not simply what we want to hear.

Phonetically, eisegesis sounds like eye-sa-G-sus, so I remember its meaning by thinking, "I, I, I, me, me, me." Again, making the text say what *I* want it to say. Lubeck says, "We must give our utmost attention to what God has written to us and how He has chosen to say it. Bible reading should be about receiving what God has given rather than "getting from it" what appeals to us."49

This is yet another good reason why it's best to start by asking Holy Spirit to speak to us through the text, to tell us what He means by it, and to ask how He intends to shape us more into His likeness through it. The full value of the Scriptures is seen when we allow Holy Spirit to lead us back to the heart of our Father through the text. To read for the sake of studying and not encountering is like running on a treadmill next to a beautiful park with trails.

It's close, but there's more available to us.

There's always more available to us.

Smith Wigglesworth, in his book *Ever Increasing FAITH*, says:

"What is still more important is for us every moment to be making an advancement in God. Looking at the Word of God today I find that its realities are greater to me today than they were yesterday. It is the most sublime, joyful truth that God brings an enlargement. Always an enlargement. There is nothing dead, dry or barren in this life of the Spirit; God is always moving us on to something higher, and as we move on in the Spirit our faith will always rise to the occasion as different circumstances arise."

Here's an easy outline you can use to practice reading the Scriptures well. It may help you get started each morning (or whatever time you

give to being in the Scriptures) as you prioritize knowing the Father, Jesus, and Holy Spirit through the Bible.
Start by writing this on your page:

S

O

A

P

Then, slowly work through each one.

Here's what they mean:

Scripture

Read it. I find some sort of plan helps me stay consistently engaged in reading the Scriptures. The Bible app on your phone or iPad has tons of them. Try asking a friend to read through the same plan with you so that you can talk about what you read, heard, and discuss how it changes your life in God today.

Observation

Jot down a few things you noticed in the text. Keep it simple, elementary, and obvious. Try for them to be seven words or less. Any observations that are longer can most likely be broken down further.

Apply

Application may be a response as you're reminded of, or noticing for the first time, something about God's character. It may lead you into a certain conversation with God, one of thanks or request or maybe repentance. Or it may be more specific, involving obedience or letting go of control of something. As you read the text, if you felt Holy Spirit telling you to do something, then now is your moment to say *yes*.

If what you heard seems odd, call a friend who is also filled with Holy Spirit. If it's from Him, and you're both open for God to reveal the value, then my guess is He will. If you hear something that doesn't line up with the character of God, reject it. Then I'd suggest praying with someone to ask for God to tell you the truth about it.

"True prophecy, as it comes forth in the power of the Spirit of God, will neither take from nor add to the Scriptures, but will intensify and quicken that which already has been given to us of God. The Holy Ghost will bring to our remembrance all the things that Jesus said and did. True prophecy will bring forth things new and old out of the Scriptures of truth and will make them living and powerful to us." (Smith Wigglesworth: *Ever Increasing FAITH*)

Prayer

Short or long, both are great. It's about your intention and heart. Simply seek to stay constantly aware of His leading. Talk with Him about what you just read, observed, and how it can shape your next moments.

Using an easy outline like *SOAP* can be a great way to work through key concepts as you read.

You may notice that sometimes the words in your Bible are different than those in your friend's. Why is that? Answer, *versions* and *translations*... a beautiful thing. Let's take a quick look at what they are and why they're helpful.

Fresh expressions of timeless truths are like color on a canvas. From the New American Standard version to The Message translation, there are a handful of great expressions available to us today.

The Scriptures were originally written in languages very different than English. Mostly in Hebrew, Greek and Aramaic, they needed to be translated in order for English-only readers to grasp what they said. And when it comes to the process of translation, there are a few ways to go about it.

A couple years ago, while leading a serve trip in Haiti with a group of our high school students and other leaders, I was asked to teach during a Sunday gathering. This church was made up of people who mainly spoke French and Creole. I only speak English, so we had someone translate while I spoke.

I'd say something, then our Haitian friend would repeat it to the group using words they could better understand.

The translator would listen for a few seconds then rephrase what I'd said. At times, he used completely different words than I was using, but the point was clearly exchanged between myself and those listening.

In the same way, during the process of Biblical translation, certain words needed to be changed so that we could understand them. Some words don't directly exist across languages and need to be expanded upon to convey the concept. Other times, the order of words need to be rearranged to make more sense.

I say all this to shine light on the numerous decisions that get made when translating the thousands of stories, poems, songs, teachings, letters, debates, and talks which make up the Bible. The spectrum of ways to translate is wide enough that each translation or version has its own benefits. At one end is a *literal* (or formal) translation and the other, *dynamic* (or functional).

Each valid version or translation of the Bible draws from the same original texts, but as we're beginning to see, the way each translation team went about putting it in English may have been very different. On the *literal* end of the spectrum, the translators exchanged *word for word*. The benefit of this translation style is its accuracy to the original words. The drawback can be that the words may be in an order uncommon to us today.

This is why I was never very good at Spanish. I knew what the words meant, but I'd put them in the same order as English, which would result in saying something funny. It sounded like broken English, understandable, but not pretty.

At the other end of the spectrum is a *dynamic* translation which is similar to what our friend in Haiti was doing as I spoke. This way of going about it focuses more on *idea for idea*. So you get the thoughts, but technically it's not word for word from the text.

There are benefits at both ends and of everything in-between.

A more literal translation is great for studying the Scriptures, while a more dynamic translation is easier to read and comprehend quickly.

Here are some of the more common translations available. You'll notice the *NIV* is near the middle. It's a good balance between literal and dynamic translations, which is why I chose to use it throughout this book. Since *The Message* is on the more dynamic end of translations, it's brilliant at getting to the heart of the text which is why in certain places I used it to avoid getting caught up on words we don't hear in our everyday conversations.

Literal translation (Word for word)

New American Standard Version (NASB)

English Standard Version (ESV)

New International Version (NIV)

The Passion Translation

New Living Translation (NLT)

The Message

Dynamic translation (Idea for idea, or paraphrase)

If you're interested in checking out any of these translations, they're available for free (except for the Passion Translation which is available on iBooks and Amazon) on *biblegateway.com* and even offline in YouVersion's Bible app.

May you know more of what God is like, growing in love, as you spend time in the Scriptures while being taught by Holy Spirit.

The Ongoing "Yes"

All growing relationships require some form of ongoing back and forth interaction. You talk… I listen. I go this way, you walk alongside.

There's a pulsing rhythm to which a healthy life is set. An interconnectedness and dependence between all living things. So too, with God I think a big part of a healthy rhythm is an ongoing "yes."

In 2 Kings we read a story about a guy named Naaman.

Naaman had a unique issue, leprosy; which was basically fatal at that point in time. The odds of recovery were slim to none and instead of a hospital bed, society would kick you out of your house, away from your family and from everything you knew, making you live in a camp outside the city filled with people who also had leprosy. The intention was good, to keep others from contracting the disease, but the emotional effects for the outcast must have been devastating. People would literally make an effort to avoid you. In some places, you'd even have to yell out, "untouchable" or "diseased one" as you walked around so people knew you were "dirty."

Not a great way to live. It's clear Naaman had a pressing need in his life.

As the story unfolds, a girl working for the family speaks up telling Naaman about a prophet who lives in a nearby city. Back in these days, God choose to primarily speak through a particular person who would then tell everyone what God said. They called these people "prophets," or "seers." So Naaman quickly packs his bags and hits the road in hopes of meeting this guy. He assumes if this prophet could interact with God, that maybe He could "get direct access to God." Direct access to healing.

When he shows up at the prophet's house. He knocks, or yells out "hello," or whatever they'd do to let him know he was there. Then he waits.

Verse nine of chapter five gives us such a profound insight into how to start a conversation with God (in this case with the prophet because it was how he'd speak to God). It says, "So Naaman went with his horses and chariots and stopped at the door of Elisha's (the Prophet) house.

Notice, he *stopped*.

That little word, "stopped," is key.

When you stop and wait at someone's door, you're completely dependent on them to answer it. After all, you're engaging them in hopes for a response. He knew where the answer would come from and was willing to look nowhere else.

As the story continues, the camera stays on Naaman as he waits on the prophet's front porch desperate for an answer, or direction, or something. He just waits... I can only imagine it was a bit uncomfortable as thoughts of doubt must have been begging for his attention. But he waited in the silence none the less.

Naaman eventually gets a response, but a very different one than he assumed. Elisha says, "Go, wash yourself seven times in the Jordan, and your flesh will be restored and you will be cleansed."
2 Kings 5v10b

Naaman instantly gets frustrated, rejecting the word because he expected Elisha to wave a magic wand and heal him:

"But Naaman went away angry and said, "I thought that he would surely come out to me and stand and call on the name of the Lord his God, wave his hand over the spot and cure me of my leprosy." 2 Kings 5v11

Funny how sometimes God tells us to do things we don't understand, but I think these moments are more for us than for Him. They create an opportunity for our value system to be reset. In Naaman's case, he may have been willing to obey the big picture (wash in a river), but when it came to the specific (the *Jordan* river) he said *no*.

"Are not Abana and Pharpar, the rivers of Damascus, better than all the waters of Israel? Couldn't I wash in them and be cleansed?" So he turned and went off in a rage." 2 Kings 5v12

So Naaman put it off, choosing pride and anger over obedience. Time passes, but his situation stays the same. He continues to suffer while the people around him encourage him to believe and obey God for what He'd said. Yet even in his stubbornness, God's promise to him didn't go anywhere.

What God said was patiently waiting to be fulfilled.

The same opportunity to listen and obey is available to us today. And now is the moment to say *yes*. His words are always for our best.

Eventually Naaman says yes, but not without a ton of drama and unnecessary pain. God was patient through his processing and pleased when Naaman opened himself up to believing.[50] The implications of him listening, but not obeying, could have resulted in never getting healed. Yet his entire reality changed because he accepted and believed (which resulted in obeying) what God had spoken to him.

I think there's always an opportunity for us to move forward in this place. We can ask and listen, but then we move into the territory of waiting.

Sometimes waiting may be the first step, while on other days it's the second or third. The process is relational and fluid, so the point here is simply to recognize the power and value of waiting. You'll know when it's best to wait.

Has God spoken something to you in the past that you've set aside? How could saying *yes* change your relationship with Him? How could it advance your level of willingness to trust Him moving forward? Can you trust that what He's asking is for your best? Take a minute to have a conversation with Him about whatever you feel He may be speaking to you, then jot down what you hear:

It's easy to look back on situations that were at one time overwhelming and think how much easier they would have been if we knew then what we know now. How much of the fear of saying *yes* is only a shadow? Something we're convinced is more difficult, powerful, and real than it really is? The trust of saying *yes to God* is believing that He sees the other side and is inviting us into a better outcome than we could imagine.

You can trust Him.

By saying *yes*, we become more aligned with the heart of God. We become more capable of living outside our small opinions and shift into a perspective that's based on wanting heaven to come into the situations we're part of. We begin asking for the same things He wants as they start becoming reality.

When we choose to live with the attitude and spirit of an *ongoing yes* we're gaining the ability to be more synced with God, more aligned... and in the end our capacity to receive His blessing is expanded.

God likes to do things that are so complex that there's no logical way we can take credit for them. These moments remind us He's involved, close, and has insight above and beyond ours. The impossible things can change because we're asking questions in line with who He is and what He wants. Saying *yes* is the faith part of life with God. Saying *yes* is believing.

If you want to see incredible things happen, position yourself to listen, wait, then say *yes*.

His way is always the best way.

But what about the times when you don't "have a word"? What if God isn't asking you to do something specific right now? Well, for starters, I think there will be changing seasons of conversation with God. And that's great. Keep this in your back pocket until you need it.

Sometimes we hear His voice in certain ways more than others. No two relationships are identical. If they were, life would be rather boring. Know that the way He speaks with you is unique and beautiful and something to be celebrated.

As you continue learning what it looks like to hear God's voice, remember He'll communicate in ways you can understand. His goal isn't to be tricky, rather it's when we compare the way we each hear from God that it gets messy. You're free in God to hear from Him the way He wants to communicate with you.

I have a good friend who interacts with God through color. Another through words. Another through pictures. Another through music. Another through art. Another through exercise. Another through other cultures. Another through the outdoors. Another through reading. Another through dancing. Another through people in need. And the list goes on. God knows what will get our attention and get the message across. **The question isn't so much, "Is God speaking?," but "Are we listening?"**

There's no shortage of ways He speaks. Start each day by relaxing, breathing deep, reminding yourself that because of Jesus you're safe in

God. Always start in relationship. The conversational access you have is the bedrock to life in God and the greatest reality of life.

Smith Wigglesworth, one of my heroes, gently reminds us, "Do not seek the gifts unless you are purposed to abide in the Holy Spirit."[51] And while this is in context to stuff the Spirit does, it applies to all things in our life with God. We could reiterate his statement by saying, *don't get caught up in hearing from God if you're unwilling to just be with Him.*

So be in the Scriptures often. Thank Him for being with you and ask Him to make something stand out to show you more of who He is. I'd suggest committing to regular reading, especially when we don't feel like it, is another form of waiting on the Lord (regardless of whether it's a little or a lot. And, even still, He may give you a line that sustains you for many days.)

When you recognize Holy Spirit speaking (whether through the Scriptures, nature, people, art, music, exercising, etc.) ask Him what it means *for you.* Not in a relative way, but a next step way. What does it mean for you to accept, absorb, and adopt His words to you? Is there an action to take? A decision to make? A start or an end to establish?

Saying *yes* to God is always the start to something great because His perspective is established in deep love, adoration, and longing to bless. He actually *wants* to bless you.

If nothing stands out, jot down a few lines as a summary and share it with someone. Be okay with asking questions. Constantly remind yourself that He's with you as you continue in the process of allowing God to expand the vocabulary He uses with you, being open to *when* and *how* He speaks.

Personally, I spend a few minutes each day writing. It's what works for me. Anytime I feel like God may be speaking, I mark it with a star and circle so that I can quickly revisit it later. At the end of each year, or when a notebook is full, I flip through it, reading all the marked moments. It's amazing seeing the themes God was talking with me about as I step back and read through them all together. Themes I had completely missed in the day-to-day moments.

—

Rhythm of Practicing Peace

Take some time to work through the next three questions as you read from Matthew 9v27-30a:

1. "As Jesus went on from there, two blind men followed him, calling out, "Have mercy on us, Son of David!"

These guys were unwilling to leave until Jesus responded to them. How often do I pray, then assume God doesn't want to speak to me because I don't hear anything within 30 seconds? These men were passionate about getting a response from God, unwilling to stop until they heard His voice. What would it look like if in my times with God in the Scriptures, I didn't get up until I got a word (something to stand out) from the Lord? If this is difficult, why?

2. "When he had gone indoors, the blind men came to him, and he asked them, "Do you believe that I am able to do this?" "Yes, Lord," they replied."

They. Faith is multiplied by being around other people who acknowledge the same need to see something miraculous happen in their life. If you're at a difficult place in life, what steps could you take to find other people who are in a similar spot seeking the same healing from Jesus?

3. "Then he touched their eyes and said, "According to your faith let it be done to you..." and their sight was restored."

"Restored," meaning something they once had was taken from them or lost, but now it's theirs again. What lack in your life has God spoken to you about, and how does believing He can restore it change the way you see that part of your life right now? What does it look like to live in faith today that His word is the coming reality as you choose to say *yes* to Him?

—

Psalm 38 outlines a few areas of life where we, like Naaman, can find ourselves feeling trapped. It's in these moments where saying *yes* to God becomes most real... and often most difficult.

Guilt

"There is no soundness in my bones because of my sin.
My guilt has overwhelmed me
like a burden too heavy to bear."

Physical and Emotional Health

"My wounds fester and are loathsome
because of my sinful folly.
I am bowed down and brought very low;
all day long I go about mourning.
My back is filled with searing pain;
there is no health in my body.
I am feeble and utterly crushed;"

Heartache

"I groan in anguish of heart."

Depression and Anxiety

"All my longings lie open before you, Lord;
my sighing is not hidden from you.
My heart pounds, my strength fails me;
even the light has gone from my eyes."

Loneliness and Paranoia

"My friends and companions avoid me because of my wounds;
my neighbors stay far away.
Those who want to kill me set their traps,
those who would harm me talk of my ruin;
all day long they scheme and lie.
I am like the deaf, who cannot hear,
like the mute, who cannot speak;
I have become like one who does not hear,
whose mouth can offer no reply."

But in all this... David pauses in verse fifteen, quieting himself saying:

"LORD, I wait for you;
you will answer, Lord my God."

He was at a split in the road and had a choice to make. His attention
and thoughts, and therefore his trust, was about to be directed down
one of two paths. The first was to focus on his very real issues in life in
that moment. The second was to remind himself of who God was and
wait for Him to speak.

He committed to the latter. Choosing to declare who God was and who
He'll continue to be for him even though He may have felt a million miles
away. This didn't undermine the seriousness of David's situation, but it
shifted his reliance from himself onto God.

"LORD, I wait for you;
you will answer, Lord my God."

The all caps "LORD" refers to YHWH, or the Creator. David knew God wasn't far away, but close and knowable.[52] From that place, he was able to remind himself, *out loud* of who YHWH was, and who He was for him.

You may find it helpful to write out a phrase you can return to in the moments of feeling hopeless that remind you of God's goodness. Something like, "He is for me! Always faithful to me! Gracious to me! Compassionate to me! Patient with me! So patient with me! He's here with me now. Yes, yes, yes. God, I'm set on waiting for You to answer me. I put my trust in You believing You are good!"

Our words have the ability to redirect our emotions. They can reframe our circumstances, giving us a new perspective of what's right in front of us.

Through God's words, space and time came into being. Through words, we declare that Jesus is King and we're welcomed into His family.[53] Through words, we build each other up and tear each other down. And it's through a word from God, as we grab onto it, that our entire reality can shift in a moment.

Words are a big deal, and here David grounds his wavering emotions with solid words. He reminds himself that "his best" is waiting for God to be God. Not allowing the tapes of *what could be* or *what was* to play on repeat in his mind… but to wait on the LORD.

So in moments of deep discouragement, when you feel guilty, when you get sick, when you feel depressed and down and worrying is the most tempting option, when your friends bail on you and fall through… pull your Bible out and have an honest dialogue with God. Engage Him in Spirit and in truth. Grab your notebook, read out loud all the times He's come through for you in the past. Verbally create an atmosphere of faith by reading out loud *your* star and circle moments, those things you wrote down and marked because you felt God was speaking to you.

Revisit them, meditate on them, and trust that He's given you everything you need to make it through that moment.

And be with people, because we need each other.

Matthew 9 says, "*they* called out," "*they* came to Him," "*they* responded," "Jesus touched *their* eyes," "*their* sight was restored." Do you see it? Our faith grows and is strengthened by being *with* others. These two guys were in the midst of terrible pain and hurt, but in honesty and vulnerability, they refused to pretend to have it all together.

Today, I think if we were in that situation, we'd introduce ourselves and ask how long the other had been blind, not mentioning that we were blind too. After all... how would they know? Then we'd go on with our day completely missing a deep and powerful friendship rooted in a common need for the manifestation of God's glory through healing.

But these two were healed because they decided to go after Jesus *together*, to be restored, and made whole *together*. They refused to stand up tall and continue bumping into things getting bruised and cut. Pride can entice us to miss what God wants to do *in* and *through* our lives.

The story says they "followed Him (Jesus), calling out..."

That word *calling* is the same word used in Matthew 14 when the disciples were in a boat during a storm and were crying out in fear, and then again as the writer explains how Peter felt:

"But when he saw the wind, he was afraid and, beginning to sink, cried out, "Lord, save me!" (v30)

That's what these two blind men were doing. They were desperate, with no other options. Remember, worry leads us into an even darker place, but crying out to our Father and believing what He says really is the best thing. My buddy Matt says it like this, "The moment we start worrying is the moment we forget who God is."

I like that.

We can't wholeheartedly believe two opposing things at once. And someone who chooses to live with an ongoing *yes to God* mentality is constantly making an effort to remember, "God *will* answer. He *is* who He says He is. I don't *have to* worry, instead I *get to celebrate* the breakthrough up ahead!"

This is what believing the Gospel does, it allows us to live full of hope for what's right around the corner.

"For I hope (to wait, to expect), in You, O LORD; You will answer, O Lord my God." Psalm 39v7 (NASB)

Have you ever looked forward to a day?

A certain event or birthday?

A trip?

I remember surprising my wife Hillary with a trip to Hawaii... on the way to the airport! She had no idea (so I'd like to think). But the days leading up to the trip seemed like forever. They couldn't go by fast enough!

David says, *I can't wait for...* catch this, "*You,* O LORD." He was so expectant and hopeful for Jesus to be made known in that moment that he couldn't sit still.

What would it look like for us to have that kind of attitude and emotion toward the ugly situations we're in right now?

May you know that God *will* restore all the broken parts of your life. That He has not forgotten you, and that He feels what you feel. That you will again know joy, hope, and victory in all areas of your life. And may you choose to wait for Him, taking on the attitude and spirit of *an ongoing yes to His voice.*

Is One Sin Worse Than Another?

This past summer, I took a handful of young people and college aged leaders down to Crater Lake for a few days in hopes to pull away from the over-connectedness of our culture and just breathe again. We spent time talking face to face, building fires (which for young guys, is the closest thing to heaven they know), reading and discussing the teachings of Jesus, eating together, and of course hiking. But one of the most amazing moments for me took place mid-morning on our second day. We ran into a leader from another one of our churches in Portland.

We're 183 miles from home, in the middle of a forest, no cell signal, and we bump into someone we know. And even more mindblowing was what he was doing in Crater Lake.

He said he was "running the Pacific Crest Trail for a few weeks."

What!? I clarified, and yes, he said *running*.

During the day, he ran. During the nights, he'd wrap himself in a tiny heat blanket (which looked like a roll of tin foil), sleep, then get back up and keep going. He carried a tiny pack that held little to nothing and would find food along the way.

This guy was running for hours on end, sometimes not seeing people for days. What a stud!

Now imagine he's moving at a good pace from point A towards point B and gets hurt. He steps on a log the wrong way and breaks his ankle. Once he got healthy again, he would have to train a second time if he wanted to finish what he'd started.[54] He'd be entering a whole new process, one he'd already gone through, but one that'd be necessary in order to give it another go.

Similarly, as we continue to move from thinking and relating to God as *god,* into calling Him *our Abba,* there are mindsets to be cautious of which can take us "back" into the former mindsets of seeing God as far away. One of those moments is how we answer the question, "Is one sin worse than another?" Our response to this question helps identify what we think about ourselves and those around us. It's not uncommon to use this question as a comparison guide to establish who we think is *more* valuable and who we think is *less.* It can lead us to thinking someone is *dirty,* or that we're *better* than someone else. **But a healthy approach to this question can lead us to value people the way God does, wanting to see them set free more than wanting to see them punished.**

This question has the potential to shape our expression of life with God and each other in massive ways. It can be the catalyst for a religious spirit, judgmental attitude, or critical outlook on life. Or... it can be a constant reminder that living in a free and spacious place is our home. Heaven now.

So why do we use this question as a hidden standard by which to measure the people around us?

I wonder if it has to do with what it offers us… levels. And by levels, I mean a system of hierarchy in which we build a *mirage of control* over one another. A subtle comparison, so focused on issues, that we fall into the trap of creating prisons for one another because of a lack of our own identity.

John 8v1-11 may be my favorite story in the Gospels, if not the entire Bible:

"Jesus went to the Mount of Olives. At dawn he appeared again in the temple courts, where all the people gathered around him, and he sat down to teach them. The teachers of the law and the Pharisees brought in a woman caught in adultery. They made her stand before the group and said to Jesus, "Teacher, this woman was caught in the act of adultery. In the Law Moses commanded us to stone such women. Now what do you say?" They were using this question as a trap, in order to have a basis for accusing him. But Jesus bent down and started to write on the ground with his finger. When they kept on questioning him, he straightened up and said to them, "Let any one of you who is without sin be the first to throw a stone at her." Again he stooped down and wrote on the ground. At this, those who heard began to go away one at a time, the older ones first, until only Jesus was left, with the woman still standing there. Jesus straightened up and asked her, "Woman, where are they? Has no one condemned you?" "No one, sir," she said. "Then neither do I condemn you," Jesus declared. "Go now and leave your life of sin."

The Pharisees couldn't have been more clear. They verbally identified themselves as ones who assumed their sin was less "bad" than this lady's sin. But were they correct in thinking so? I mean they had a pretty good case for punishment right?

Jesus seemed to disagree. He offered a third way of looking at the situation, turning the attention from the woman to the group, identifying *everyone* there as on the "same level."

Thinking this way forces us to think about *why* we're asking this question in the first place. Is it possible they were asking it in hopes to feel better about themselves? As if to say, *she's worse than us... so that makes us better than her.*

If so, that's a dangerous place to live from. Jesus makes that super clear. This kind of attitude nearly caused a woman to die so that others could feel "right."

When we choose to live with this kind of attitude towards each other, righteousness is assumed to be derived from ourselves being *better* than others, rather than from Jesus.

You've probably heard some of Jesus' most famous words in Matthew 5. Words like, "You have heard that it was said, 'You shall not commit adultery.' But I tell you that anyone who looks at a woman lustfully has already committed adultery with her in his heart." He's quoted saying a ton of these kinds of statements. But what is He saying?

Basically… 1 =1. Or, sin = sin.

Now, without argument, some sin (that is, choosing to act on desires that are contrary to God's best for us) has more immediate and impacting consequence than others. As an example, injustice is injustice, but greater injustice has a greater effect. I think we can all agree that *imagining* to punch someone in the face has less outward consequence than *actually* punching them. Sure, but ultimately every sin is *us opposing God*. Regardless of whether we consider it "big" or "small."

So maybe "little" or "big" isn't the point. And what if the outward action of sin isn't the core issue either? What if any given "moment of sin" is a byproduct of operating out of *fear* rather than *Love*? What if our most real issue is simply remaining *in His love*?

When the Scriptures use this concept of *remaining in God's love*, it's not referring to the emotional feelings of being "in love" with someone as much as it's a location phrase. It's an atmosphere thing. It explains your surroundings. The atmosphere in my favorite coffee shop makes me feel a certain way. It's clean, yet comfortable, which allows me to relax and focus on whatever I'm working on. It's filled with natural light, yet balanced with cool tones, which is constantly reverting my attention to outside and onto how complex nature is. My surroundings produce feelings. Not the other way around. *In God* is a reality phrase intended to paint a picture to remind us of what's most true. Us *in God*.

Or, *in Love*.
So what if the main issue in the garden story of Genesis wasn't the visible act of them sinning, as much as humanity choosing to momentarily reject living in Love? And instead, choosing to live in fear?

What if *fear* is the root of all sin, therefore the bigger issue?

And what if every second of every minute, of every hour, of every day we *only* face the decision to live *in fear* or to live *in Love*?

God isn't afraid of our sinful actions. He's past our sin and wants us to get past it too. There's no need for us to fixate on it anymore. He desires for us to live free *in Love*, all attention and energy directed there, not at fighting wrong urges.

What if living *in Love* is more powerful, real, and important than focusing on not to doing certain things... sinning?

In Colossians 1v13-14, Paul explains there are two kingdoms... which is to say, there's no middle ground. Everything fits somewhere. This means off-ness from God is off-ness from God.

Like a seed, a thought grows into an action, which turns into a habit, which matures into an addiction (or pattern or rhythm). I think this is what Jesus may have been referring to with the story of the woman in John 8. Before you *do*, you've entertained the idea, which means you're already there on the inside. It just hasn't manifested on the outside yet. But because we love systems and concrete ways of explaining things, we like to place every sin (of us and others) on a scale.

Welcome to the sin gauge. It quietly hangs on the walls of our thinking:

1   2   3   4   5   6   7   8   9   10

A Thought: "Not that bad"   *An Action: "Really bad"*

So is a thought worse than an action? Is one sin really worse than another?

While there are different physical outcomes, I'm not sure we can ask this question without still having an agenda of attempting to create a level system... the very system Jesus seemed to want to get away from. Jesus introduced a new way of thinking which results in a new way of living. A correct and more simple way to think about sin. To Jesus, all of humanity is (or was) far from God.

"All have sinned and fall short of the glory of God," Romans 3v23. Which is to say we're all in this together. Every person on the planet at one time was separated from life with God. Many still are. But the verse continues, "and all are justified freely by His grace through the redemption that came by Christ Jesus... to be received by faith." Romans 3v24

In other words, Jesus is the door to all that is God. And He says (my words), "Come on in, welcome home friend, let's celebrate! All you have to do is receive it, just show up!"

This means there's hope. There's *always* hope because of Jesus. That's His heart for you, to be *full* of hope. When we recognize and receive who He wants to be for us, fear becomes a lot less appealing. It's in this place where the question of *which sin is worse* dissolves. It's just not an issue for humanity to carry. Rather, we begin entertaining a different question, a better question:

What does it look like to live *in Love* today? To express His love and grace and invitation to everyone around me?

I'm aware this may sound elementary, but by returning to our intended position of enjoying God as our Father, there's no room for comparison or judgement between His kids. That's God's place, not ours. Sin has consequences, sure. But even when we correct each other, the goal is repentance by reminder of who God says we are so that His kindness comes back into view. It's His kindness that will lead us to choose repentance. We'll *want* to return.

1 John 4v13-19 is brilliant. If you want a tattoo, here's a good one:

"This is how we know that we live in him and he in us: He has given us of his Spirit. And we have seen and testify that the Father has sent his

Son to be the Savior of the world. If anyone acknowledges that Jesus is the Son of God, God lives in them and they in God. And so we know and rely on the love God has for us. God is love.

Whoever *lives in love lives in God, and God in them*.

This is how love is made complete among us so that we will have confidence on the day of judgment: In this world we are like Jesus.

There is no fear in love. But perfect love drives out fear, because fear has to do with punishment. The one who fears is not made perfect in love.

We love because he first loved us."

We can be *in God*, but choose to give our attention to fear (in this case, a level system) which pulls our "give and take" active engagement *from God* and offers it to people. Then, in order to stay stable, we have to keep everyone around us in check. The comparison game is a balancing act. This is how the Pharisee's (unfortunately) are often painted in the Scriptures... as playing catch up. **They lived in fear, which turned to control, which resulted in anger and judgement.**

Remember what Jason Upton said? "Love is a dangerous word to those who fear losing control."[55]

Yes, yes, yes. Ultimately, *every* decision we make comes down to being *in Love* or *in fear*.

We rarely see a recorded instance in the Scriptures of the Pharisees (minus Nicodemus) conversationally asking God what He thought about a situation. Sure they knew God's story, but did they bother to talk with Him? In most of the stories, they acted from what they thought they knew about God, their interpretations. In fear, there was no other way to interpret the Scriptures than what they'd been taught. But knowledge and active relationship are two different things[56] and Jesus had come to be the fulfillment and fullness of God's story (specifically the Law.)

So, all of humanity was sinful (or far from God), but Jesus made a way for us to be holy no matter how "big" we think the sin is, to be made close to Him again. And as always, the goal isn't to know this stuff, but to live it.

When I want to judge someone... what am I afraid of? How am I wanting "to be God" in that moment? We judge people because we don't have control over the outcome, the pain, the mess that now is, or whatever it may be. That lack of control is an uncomfortable place to be, usually leading to fear and then the attempt to gain control. But it's God's job to restore, to clean up the mess, and to heal the situation or relationship. So in the end, our attempt to be God is done out of fear knowing we cannot be God. Funny huh?

Oh how the enemy wants us to stay confused, like a hamster running on a wheel… continuing to do the same things over and over, getting nowhere.

May we know that *in God*,

in Love,

the place we are,

that fear does not exist.

That we're free from having to be in control or needing to express judgement on ourselves or others. It's God's space, not ours. And that the greatest place to live from is remembering we are safe, secure, loved, and free from accusation or having to judge everyone around us.

Along the way, watch for this. It will come up, and when it does… you know what to do.

Rhythm of Practicing Peace

Take a minute to process through what all this means for your life today.

Ask: Is there someone I'm holding in judgement? If so, what am I afraid of? How am I trying to be God in that relationship?

If Holy Spirit is speaking to you now, take a deep breath in and respond to Him. Write out their names and the root of the issue, then ask God to help you release your control of them

Be honest, He loves that.

Epilogue

What are a few things that stuck out to you as you read this book?

Go back through the *Rhythms of Practicing Peace* and look for a theme or common idea that runs through your responses. If you recognize one, keep the conversation (about that idea or theme) open and active with God and others. He may want to do more for you in that area of your life.

The way of Jesus, and learning to enjoy Jesus, is one of grace and rest. This was His way in Genesis 1-2 long before life spiraled into chaos, and it continues to be His way through Revelation 22, the bliss of the new heavens and new earth.

He's the ultimate protector, provider, comforter, teacher, nurturer, friend, and everything else we long for in its purity. He is always faithful and the Savior of everyone who seeks and receives Him as the great Restorer of all things, starting with us. He's the patient loving King of a world that often chooses to live in rebellion because they've accepted the rumors of the enemy.

Even still, it's not uncommon to go through times of considering *giving up on faith* because of confusion, frustration, or pain. In these moments it seems easiest to toss everything "spiritual"[57] away, saying there's no way to know what's true, or to do the opposite and say it's *all* worth saying *yes* to.

If that's you, know that you're not alone.

The disciples were with Jesus for three years, God in flesh, and still didn't get it at times. So how much more room is there for *us* to ask questions?

Don't give up.

Don't toss Jesus aside.

Keep going.

In those moments, I'd encourage you to release what you think you know and read the book of John from start to finish. If you can, try to do so in one sitting. Ask Holy Sprit to speak to you and when you're done reading, write out a line or two in response to this question:

Who is Jesus?

Then share what you wrote with your closest friends, be sure to include a few who are learning what it means to be Jesus' disciples too.

At other points along the way, we get to be the ones who help those in pain and confusion. Reminding each other we're loved, that we have a place in God's family, and that one day all the pain, confusion, and hurt will be replaced with pure bliss in Jesus. His very being and goodness will permeate all things:

Everything will find its healing, meaning, and value in the light of the Lamb. "There will be no more night. They will not need the light of a lamp or the light of the sun, for the Lord God will give them light. And they will reign for ever and ever." Revelation 22v5

So may you continue on… encouraged and expectant for the next part of your journey to be the best yet. "And may the God of hope fill you with all joy and peace as you trust in Him, so that you may overflow with hope by the power of the Holy Spirit." Romans 15v13

About the Author

Nate is currently pastoring young people in Portland, Oregon and can regularly be found on the golf course or working in the yard. His wife Hillary works at Nike and enjoys running. Their dog Royal gets free reign of the house and knows the meaning of the words, "walk," "treat," and "kisses."

After a number of years teaching for Apple, and being a part of a church community of 18-26 year olds called The Way, Nate was brought on staff at Solid Rock Church (Now Westside: A Jesus Church) in 2011 and then transitioned to 26 West Church in April of 2016 as Pastor of Young People & Communications.

His goal is simple. To show, tell, and express the wonder and goodness of the Father, Son, and Holy Spirit for every person both individually and communally.

Instagram: @natekupish   **Web:** natekupish.com

Endnotes

Preface

[1] "The ark of the covenant of the Lord went before them during those three days to find them a place to rest." Numbers 10v33b. Or in other words, God's presence was ahead of them preparing a place of rest.

"Truly my soul finds rest in God…" Psalm 62v1a

[2] Peterson, Eugene H. *The Pastor: A Memoir*. New York: HarperOne, 2011.

[3] How He see's you is far more important and weighty than how you see yourself. And it's as we give our attention to Him, that His thoughts about us become more clear. He's the fulfillment to our lack, the fullness to our emptiness, and the friend we long for in each moment. "For He chose us in Him before the creation of the world to be holy and blameless *in His sight*." Ephesians 1v4

[4] "But you will not leave in haste or go in flight; for the LORD will go before you, the God of Israel will be your rear guard." Isaiah 52v12

"I look behind me and you're there, then up ahead and you're there, too – your reassuring presence, coming and going. This is too much, too wonderful – I can't take it all in!" Psalm 139v5-6 (The Message)

5 "I turned around to see the voice that was speaking to me. And when I turned I saw seven golden lamp stands, and among the lamp stands was someone like a son of man, dressed in a robe reaching down to his feet and with a golden sash around his chest. The hair on his head was white like wool, as white as snow, and his eyes were like blazing fire. His feet were like bronze glowing in a furnace, and his voice was like the sound of rushing waters. In his right hand he held seven stars, and coming out of his mouth was a sharp, double-edged sword. His face was like the sun shining in all its brilliance. When I saw him, I fell at his feet as though dead. Then he placed his right hand on me and said: "Do not be afraid. I am the First and the Last. I am the Living One; I was dead, and now look, I am alive for ever and ever! And I hold the keys of death and Hades." Revelation 1v12-18

6 My friend Karlee calls this the "love seat," not the "trouble seat." I like that.

What Happened?

7 While God isn't confined to time or space, we are. So God always was, but creation fits in time and space, meaning we have a start. Science and God are often thought to clash, but they don't. Science and people's thinking of God clash, sure… all the time. I'm pretty sure we're not always right nor do we have it all figured out. And that's okay. It's okay to say, "I don't know." Science acts as a lens to better know the wonder of God. The issue isn't how many years the world has been around, it's stepping back to see that God is bigger than our assumptions and equations.

8 Genesis 1 and Hebrews 11v3 are both welcome statements to the story of God and life as we know it. Here's the Hebrews one… "By faith we understand that the universe was formed at God's command, so that what is seen was not made out of what was visible."

[9] "He" simply implies a *being* rather than a *force* or a *thing*. Both male and female are created from what God is like. They resemble *God*. Therefore God is neither male nor female, but male and female are parts of what God is like.

Both male and female are created in Their (Father, Jesus, and Holy Spirit) image. Our nature is created for community just like God is in Himself a community. We use the word *He* most often in referring to God because it helps our minds shape as much of God as we can grasp into a relational being.

That's one of the reasons Jesus is so incredible. He was God, and therefore showed us what God is like, but also exhibited assumed characteristics of both male and female such as authority and compassion. I'm not attempting to touch the gender roles concept here, only making the point that God is not an old guy in the sky with a beard.

"Then God said, "Let us make mankind in our image, in our likeness… So God created mankind in his own image, in the image of God he created them; male and female he created them." Genesis 1v26-27

[10] If you stood in front of me and your friend stood behind, the way you'd explain what I look like would be both similar and unique based on your perspectives.

[11] Sky and earth. Light and color. Water and air. Gravity and physics. Vegetation and animals.

[12] While the snake isn't named at this point in the story, Genesis 3v14-15 is a prophecy, or look forward, to what will happen to the snake one day. And in Revelation 12v9, we see the connection between the snake and the fallen Angel named Lucifer, now called Satan, "The great dragon was hurled down – that ancient serpent called the devil, or Satan, who leads the whole world astray. He was hurled to the earth, and his angels with him."

[13] Why human? Satan pushed against God and all He is… that includes life and His creation. As His creation, animated by His life, the enemy hates us too. But life, and love, wins.

[14] Real love doesn't force itself on the other, it let's them choose. My Mom explained it to me years ago through a picture. She said, "If you squeeze a bird in your hand because you're worried about it flying away, it will die. But if you open your hand, giving it room to live, even if it flies away, it will return because it knows your hand is safe."

[15] "Look at me. I stand at the door. I knock. If you hear me call and open the door, I'll come right in and sit down to supper with you…" Revelation 3v20

[16] "The thief (the enemy) comes only to steal and kill and destroy; I (God in human *form*, Jesus) have come that they may have life, and have it to the full." John 10v10

[17] Graham Cooke's teaching, *Living Your Truest Identity* works through this, and a handful of other great ideas in detail.

Moving From god to Abba

[18] Everything has the potential to remind us of something. Our senses take in the details all around us and our minds express its place in our world. We can instantly be *taken back* to a moment in our past by a smell, taste, etc. And part of God making the universe physical, I believe, is so that all good things would remind us of who He is for us. Breathing is an elemental rhythmic structure, a reminder if you will, that our identity is to constantly flow *from God, to God*. With each inhale and exhale, a reminder of His nearness and love.

[19] We know what God is like by looking at Jesus, "…to see me is to see the Father…" John 14v9. And I believe we get glimpses of His goodness through each other, unity from unity. But to fully base what He's like off of someone other than Jesus is not a complete picture and can become "a human identity ceiling on a supernatural God."

[20] "This righteousness from God comes through faith in Jesus Christ to all who believe. There is no difference, for all have sinned and fall short of the glory of God, and are justified freely by his grace through the redemption that came by Messiah Jesus." Romans 3v22-24

Relationship to Worship

[21] Jesus explains repentance in Luke 15v11-32 through a story of a son who runs from the goodness of his loving Father only to find lack. In the boy's repentance, he returns home and is welcomed not with shame and guilt, but with celebration, grace, and identity.

[22] "I have swept away your offenses like a cloud, your sins like the morning mist. Return to me, for I have redeemed you." Isaiah 44v22

[23] What we often refer to as "church," but this too is something that shrinks our view of life with God. "Church" is the collective people of God, or God's family. So the gathering then, is a moment where we come together to remind each other who He is for us, directing our attention and worship toward Him as a community, and on and on. The dangerous part comes when we think the gathering is somehow more holy than the rest of the week. Holy Spirit lives in us now, we are free to worship anywhere, anytime.

"Don't you know that you yourselves are God's temple and that God's Spirit dwells in your midst?" 1 Corinthians 3v16

[24] Though singing can be a form of worship... it's not *worship* by definition. So the answer to this question isn't to play "worship music" on your iPod all day, although singing is a great outward expression of an inward impression and gives space for others to join in. Personally, I worship through song often.

[25] Singing *about* God and singing *to* God can be very different, but both are valuable. Both fit into the process of life with God. No matter where you're at, you're welcome.

[26] Or at least in how we understand these words today.

27 Transliteration occurs when we write a word in the characters (letters) of our English alphabet so that we can form a pronunciation that makes sense to our minds which are tracked in a certain set of characters and sounds that associate their meaning (a language). You may have heard the word *logos* before, well that's a transliteration of the Greek word λογοσ.

28 One of my favorite people on the planet will burst out laughing without warning. At first I thought He was crazy, then I watched his life… how He loves people, how He loves God, and most of all how He lets God love Him. And at some point, I started being open to seeing more of God's joy through him. The moments of laughter were not to get attention, they were expression of the moment He was having experiencing how majestic and glorious God is. He couldn't help but laugh! I love that in God there is freedom to worship!

29 I'd encourage you to do your best to not be a distraction to others. This may mean self-control in certain moments… again, the undefined balance.

30 "In the very beginning God was already there. And before his face was his Living Expression. And this "Living Expression" was with God, yet fully God." John 1v1 (The Message)

"The Greek word used here, and the Hebraic concept conveyed, is that of being before God's face. There is no Hebrew word for presence (i.e. the presence of God), only the word *face*." Brian Simmons. The Passion Translation: *John Eternal Love*. John 1v1 and Commentary.

31 "The thief comes only to steal and kill and destroy; I (Jesus) have come that they may have life, and have it to the full." John 10v10

Worship to Receiving

32 God's space, the "place" where He fully rules and reigns. The space that is now invading earth and will one day will reclaim all of creation as its own.

33 "But my eyes are fixed on you, Sovereign Lord; in you I take refuge, do not give me over to death." Psalm 141v8

34 "More of God" meaning in awareness and experience, not a greater percentage. The "greater percentage... more of God" thought is one of the underlying ideas at the foundation of vocational dualism (meaning the *Pastor in God* has "more of God" than the *Barista in God* because of what vocation she's in.) Not true.

35 John 5v7-9 is great picture of God bringing healing in a different way than someone thought.

36 I think it's clear enough by now, but by "worship and prayer" we don't just mean "singing and quiet time." While these are expressions of worship and prayer, they're just that, expressions of both. It's a heart thing that leads to a hands thing.

37 "Be alert and of sober mind. Your enemy the devil prowls around like a roaring lion looking for someone to devour." 1 Peter 5v8

Learning to Listen

38 "Leaning back against Jesus, he asked him, "Lord, who is it?" John 13v25

39 John 13v23, 19v26, 20v2, 21v7, 21v20

40 Album: *A Table Full Of Strangers.* Song: Love Is A Winding Road.

41 We love black and white answers. We love answers for that matter. We love the illusion of having things figured out. We love accomplishing tasks and earning rewards. We love to think we can stop any habit with five quick steps, and get fit in seven fast weeks. We say we *love* everything and yet live among broken relationships.

42 There are many, but here are a few: Psalms 7, 26, and 139

Learning to Talk

[43] We need each other. Life with God is both personal and communal. It's momentary, and eternal. It's now, and historic. Life with God is always changing because as the *somethings* behind the words and experiences move from head to heart, God is again free (in our minds) to be God, no longer bound by our selfish and limited constructs. Our faith exists and is found in both a personal and communal place. I believe this is one of the beautiful facets of this ancient faith we find ourselves in.

Learning to Trust

[44] Or as my friend Tim says, "Let's eat Grandma," vs "Let's eat, Grandma."

[45] "His divine power has given us everything we need for a godly life through our knowledge of him who called us by his own glory and goodness." 2 Peter 1v3

Reading the Scriptures

[46] Starting in Genesis 12 with Abram, the Hebrew people were God's un-original plan to show the world His goodness after the mess of the fall in Genesis 3. These people, throughout history, have been referred to by a few names (The Hebrews, Israelites, and Jews.) The Torah was the bedrock of the Old Testament, now the first fives books (Genesis, Exodus, Leviticus, Numbers, Deuteronomy) in our most recognized and read ordering of the Biblical text. This was what nearly all young Jewish people grew up reading… which is why (in summary) it's sometimes referred to as the Hebrew Scriptures.

[47] God is into clear communication, it's our receiving and opinions that make it mucky sometimes.

[48] *The NIV Application Commentary* is one of the shortest and most compact tools out there for general context. *The ESV Study Bible* is larger, but also much more in depth and includes tons of details. N.T. Wright has a series of short, easy to understand, and fun to read books called *New Testament For Everyone*. And Tremper Longman III and Scot McKnight have a series of books called *The Story of God Bible Commentary* which explain what you're reading in the context of the big story of the Bible.

[49] Page twenty-two of *Read the Bible for a Change*.

The Ongoing "Yes"

[50] God is after our heart, not doing the right thing just because it's the right thing. "There was a man who had two sons. He went to the first and said, 'Son, go and work today in the vineyard.' "'I will not,' he answered, but later he changed his mind and went. "Then the father went to the other son and said the same thing. He answered, 'I will, sir,' but he did not go. "Which of the two did what his father wanted?" "The first," they answered. Jesus said to them, "Truly I tell you, the tax collectors and the prostitutes are entering the kingdom of God ahead of you. For John came to you to show you the way of righteousness, and you did not believe him, but the tax collectors and the prostitutes did. And even after you saw this, you did not repent and believe him." Matthew 21v28-32

[51] Excerpt From: Smith Wigglesworth's, *Ever Increasing FAITH*.

[52] At this point in time, Exodus 34v6-7 is one of many examples.

[53] This isn't to say someone who is mute cannot declare Jesus is King, that'd be ridiculous. It's simply noting that words are the expression of, and the action from, what we *really* believe.

Is One Sin Worse Than Another?

54 Conceptually this would be "back" because it's something he'd already completed, but really it'd be part of his future process. I say this because revisiting elementary truths of following Jesus is not necessarily going backwards, but can be a wonderful part in the process of moving forward.

55 Jason Upton. Album: *A Table Full Of Strangers*. Song: Love Is A Winding Road

56 Holy Spirit is our teacher. Alive and active. And if we're open to Him, alone and in community, He'll teach us what the Scriptures mean. This is why everything we do comes back to intimacy with the Father, Son, and Holy Spirit.

Epilogue

57 Though everything is *spiritual*, we often use this word when referring to forms of thought that speak of the deepest parts of us and the connections we can sense between all things.

Made in the USA
Monee, IL
29 April 2020

27809101R00095